CLAIRE BENTON-EVANS
BEASTLY BIBLE STORIES

The good, the bad and the deadly

2

Illustrations by Tim Benton

www.kevinmayhew.com

KM PUBLISHING

First published in Great Britain in 2014 by Kevin Mayhew Ltd
Buxhall, Stowmarket, Suffolk IP14 3BW
Tel: +44 (0) 1449 737978 Fax: +44 (0) 1449 737834
E-mail: info@kevinmayhew.com

www.kevinmayhew.com

© Copyright 2014 Claire Benton-Evans.

The right of Claire Benton-Evans to be identified as the author of this work has been asserted by her in accordance with the Copyright, Designs and Patents Act 1988.

The publishers wish to thank all those who have given their permission to reproduce copyright material in this publication.

Every effort has been made to trace the owners of copyright material and we hope that no copyright has been infringed. Pardon is sought and apology made if the contrary be the case, and a correction will be made in any reprint of this book.

All rights reserved. No part of this publication may be reproduced, stored in a retrieval system, or transmitted, in any form or by any means, electronic, mechanical, photocopying, recording, or otherwise, without the prior written permission of the publisher.

ISBN 978 1 84867 694 7
Catalogue No. 1501423

Cover design by Rob Mortonson
Illustrations by Tim Benton
Edited by Nicki Copeland
Typeset by Rob Mortonson

Printed and bound in Great Britain

CONTENTS

Dreadful Dreams

Good news, bad news – Joseph the dreamer   7

Cannibal cows – Pharaoh's bad dreams   17

The scary statue and the crazy king –
Nebuchadnezzar's nightmares   27

Right and Wrong

The fatal flood – Noah and the ark   39

Babbling builders – the Tower of Babel   47

The crucial cut – the circumcision rule   55

Sin cities – Sodom and Gomorrah   61

Laws for living – the Ten Commandments   71

Clean and unclean – rules for eating   83

Blood and guts – rules for sacrificing animals   89

Hair-raising Horror

The horrible haircut – Samson loses his strength   101

A terrible tangle – the death of Absalom   115

ABOUT THE AUTHOR

Claire loves stories and drama but she never once played the Angel Gabriel in a school Nativity play. She studied English at Oxford, where she enjoyed reading lots of very old poems about monsters, battles and God. She gets her best ideas for writing when she's walking her dog and loves living in Scotland because she likes shortbread and mountains. She lives with her husband – a minister – and three children. They all have their own big ideas about church and they dared her to write **Beastly Bible Stories**.

Details of all Claire's titles can be found on her website at:
www.clairebentonevans.com
www.kevinmayhew.com

DREADFUL DREAMS

GOOD NEWS, BAD NEWS
Joseph the dreamer

Daddy's favourite

'Dad loves me the best!' thought Joseph to himself. He was an annoyingly handsome teenage boy with big, brown eyes, a charming smile and a complicated family: he lived with his dad, Jacob, and his 11 brothers – Reuben, Simeon, Levi, Judah, Issachar, Zebulun, Dan, Naphtali, Gad, Asher and Benjamin. Joseph's mum was dead but he had three stepmothers. (Joseph also had some sisters, but the Bible doesn't bother to name more than one.) Joseph's family moved from place to place with their flocks of sheep and goats. There were always lots of chores to be done and Joseph's big brothers bossed him about. Joseph fetched and carried for them, but whenever his brothers misbehaved – when they were lazy, mean or rude – he told their dad.

'You little sneak! Telltale!' the brothers snarled at Joseph, but Joseph just smiled his most charming smile because he knew that he was special. He was his dad's favourite.

It's true – Jacob loved Joseph more than any of his other children. To prove it he gave Joseph a special coat, woven with a rainbow of different coloured threads and cut with long, elegant sleeves. It was a fine coat for an important man, a man who wanted to stand out from the crowd, a man who didn't need to roll up his sleeves to do anyone's dirty work. Joseph knew he deserved that coat and he swanned about in it all day long, showing it off to his brothers. Of course, they were jealous. They hated Joseph and didn't have a kind word to say to him.

The brothers hated Joseph even more when he told them about his dreams. 'Hey, listen to me, everyone!' he chirped. 'I had the best dream last night! I dreamt it was harvest time: there we all were, in the middle of the field, tying up sheaves of ripe corn. Suddenly, my sheaf stood up tall, all on its own, and your sheaves gathered around it. Then your sheaves of corn all bowed to mine, like mine was a king or something!'

Joseph's brothers glared at him. Levi said, 'Do you really think you're going to be the boss of us? Huh!'

But Joseph was irrepressible – you just couldn't shut him up. The next morning he chirruped, 'I had another dream last night!' Everyone groaned.

'Now, now,' said Jacob. 'Don't be mean to darling Joseph – let my boy speak. Tell us your dream, son.'

'Well,' said Joseph, 'in this dream, I was looking at the sky. It was beautiful because the sun and the moon were there at the same time, both shining down on me, and there were 11 stars in the sky. As I looked, they all bowed to me! The sun and the moon bent down towards me, and the 11 stars fell as if they were grovelling in front of me!' Joseph's 11 brothers turned red with anger and jealousy. Joseph added, 'Do you get it? 11 stars – and there's 11 of you! How cool is that!'

The brothers seethed, and even Jacob looked concerned. 'What sort of dream is that, my son? Do you mean that I'm going to bow down before you? Me and your mothers and your brothers?'

Joseph just shrugged and smiled his most winning smile. His brothers stomped off, muttering, while Jacob stroked his long grey beard and worried about his favourite boy.

Plots, lies and a blood-covered coat

One day Joseph's brothers were out with the sheep and goats. They were a long way from home and Jacob was worried about them, so he said to Joseph, 'Go and check on your brothers, will you? Make sure everything is all right.' So Joseph wandered out into the fields on his own.

Later that day, miles from home, Joseph's brothers spotted a lone figure in the distance, making his way across the fields towards them. He was wearing a colourful coat. Even at that distance, the brothers thought they recognised Joseph's arrogant swagger.

'Uh-oh,' said Reuben.

'It's the dreamer,' said Simeon.

'Daddy's boy,' said Levi.

'I'm sick of him,' said Judah.

'He gets all the attention,' said Issachar.

'And he gets away with everything,' said Zebulun.

'He needs a good kicking,' said Dan.

'That'd teach him,' said Naphtali.

'But Dad never lets us lay a finger on him,' said Gad.

'Dad's not here now, though – is he?' said Asher. There was a pause. Each brother had the same murderous thought.

'LET'S GET HIM!' agreed the brothers, grimly. 'We'll kill him and kick his body into one of these ditches. We'll tell Dad that a wild animal attacked him. So much for his big dreams!'

But Reuben, the eldest, stepped in. 'No,' he said. 'No bloodshed. Let's just dump him in that big pit over there.'

When Joseph reached his brothers, they were huddled together like a pack, with their backs to him. 'Hi guys!' he called out cheerily. His smile froze when they turned around and he saw the look on their faces.

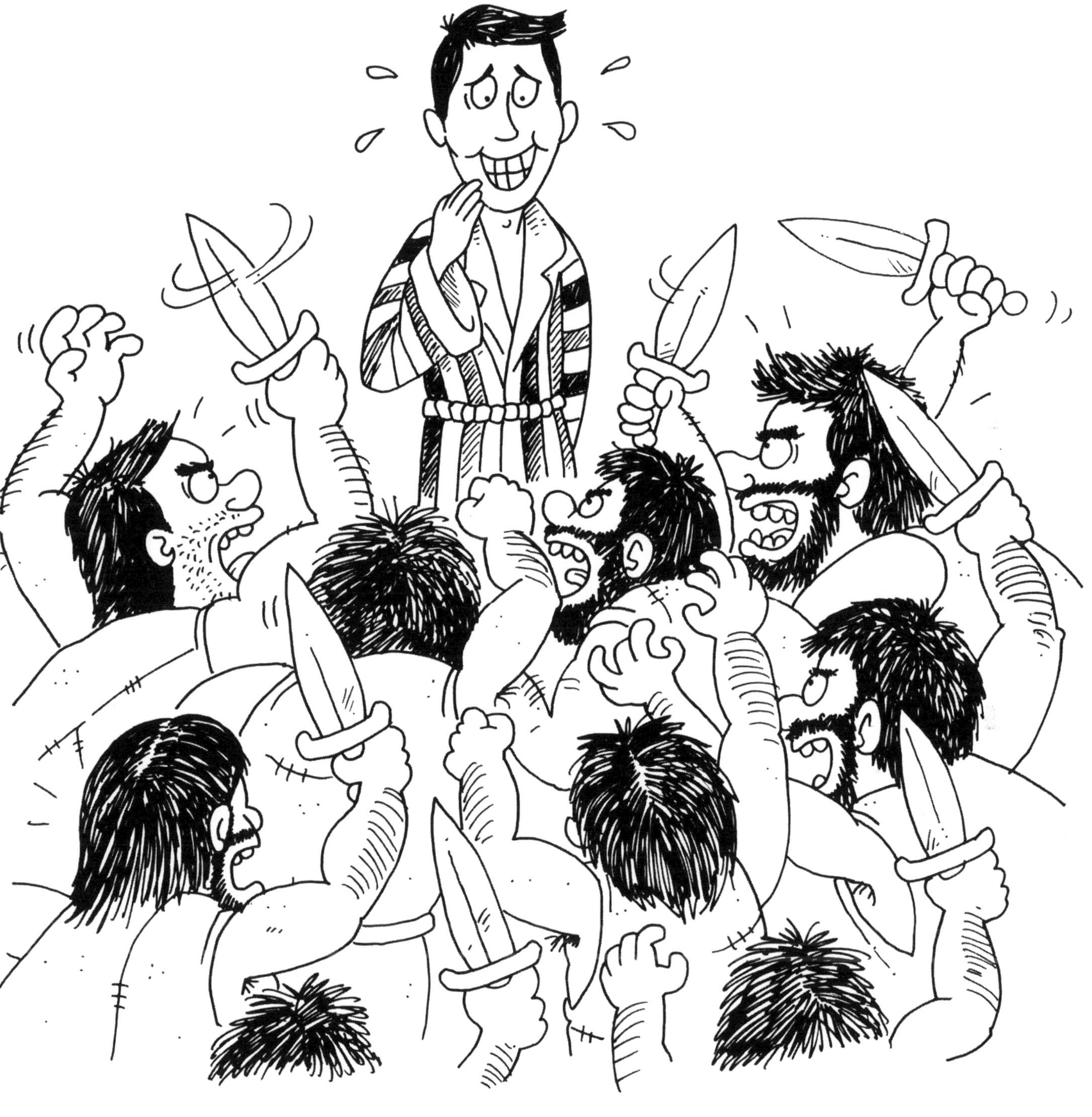

'OOOF!' The brothers collided with Joseph like a rugby scrum and knocked him to the ground.

'HELP!' he yelled, but there was no one to hear and no one to rescue him as his brothers tore off his precious coat and bundled him roughly over the edge of the pit. 'LET ME OUT!' he screamed as he scrabbled at the steep, stony sides of his prison.

The brothers got their breath back, wiped their hands and then sat down to scoff the picnic lunch they had brought with them. They guzzled water until it streamed into their beards while, a short distance away, Joseph lay in his dry pit and gasped in the sun. When they had finished eating, the brothers squinted at the horizon and spotted a group of travelling salesmen heading their way. They had camels and saddlebags loaded with loot to sell in Egypt. They gave Judah an idea: 'Hey, listen you lot – what's the point of leaving our brother here to rot when we could make some money out of him? Let's sell him!' This was a popular suggestion, so the brothers bargained with the salesmen and swapped Joseph for 20 silver coins.

As the salesmen hauled Joseph off with his hands roped behind his back, the brothers got busy. They killed one of their goats and covered Joseph's torn coat with blood, then they took it back home to Jacob with a tall story about a terrifying animal attack.

When Jacob saw the torn and bloody coat, he burst into tears and mourned the loss of his favourite son for days and days. None of his other sons or daughters could cheer him up.

Meanwhile, Joseph had arrived in Egypt and the salesmen were rubbing their hands at the thought of how much money they'd get for such a handsome lad at the slave market.

A big success

Joseph was bought by an Egyptian captain called Potiphar. God was on Joseph's side, and before long he became a trusted servant, then he was promoted; soon afterwards he became Potiphar's right-hand man. Joseph managed everything for his Egyptian master, and he did it so well that Potiphar didn't have to worry about a thing.

So Joseph became a successful man. He was also young, strong and good looking, and he caught the eye of Potiphar's bored and glamorous wife. She teased him and flirted with him, until one day she tried to kiss him. 'No!' protested Joseph. 'You're my master's wife! I'm as big a man around here as Potiphar. He's given me everything – except you, of course. Why would I cheat him?' Potiphar's wife grabbed Joseph's clothes and tried to drag him into her bedroom, but he wriggled out of his tunic and escaped.

Potiphar's wife was furious, so she made up a big lie on the spot. She showed her husband Joseph's tunic and shouted, 'Look at this! Joseph tried to kiss me, and when I shouted for help he ran away – he left this behind in my bedroom!'

'**HE DID *WHAT*?!!!**' roared Potiphar. Without stopping to hear the other side of the story, Potiphar threw Joseph in jail and left him there.

Behind bars

Joseph had lost everything – but God was on his side, and before long he became the chief jailer's trusted servant. Soon afterwards he became the jailer's right-hand man and he helped to look after the other prisoners.

Two of the prisoners in the jail had worked for Pharaoh himself. One was his head wine steward and the other was his chief baker. One night, they both had weird and vivid dreams, and they woke up in a panic. 'If only someone could tell me what my dream means!' wailed the wine steward.

'What about me?' cried the baker. 'I wish I knew what my dream says about my future!'

Joseph came and sat with them both. 'God interprets dreams,' he said. 'Tell me what you saw.'

The wine steward went first. 'Well, there was a grapevine in front of me with three branches. Suddenly, buds appeared on the vine, and as I watched they became blossoms, then the blossoms ripened into big, juicy grapes in front of my eyes. I grabbed Pharaoh's goblet, squeezed the grape juice into it and gave the goblet to Pharaoh. What does it mean?'

Joseph said, 'It's good news. The three branches mean three days: in three days' time Pharaoh will get you out of here and give you your old job back! You'll give him his wine just as you did before.' The wine steward hugged Joseph, who added, 'But please don't forget me when you're back in Pharaoh's good books. I'm stuck in this prison and I've done nothing wrong – promise you'll put in a good word for me!'

'Yeah, sure!' shouted the wine steward, who was running around the prison cell, cheering and hugging all the guards.

Then the baker tapped Joseph on the shoulder. He was keen to have some good news of his own. 'I dreamed I was carrying three baskets full of cakes and pastries on my head. In the top basket were all sorts of delicacies that I'd baked especially for Pharaoh, but the birds were eating them out of the basket. What does it mean?'

Joseph said, 'The three baskets mean three days: in three days' time Pharaoh will get you out of here – and on to the end of a hangman's rope! The birds will eat the flesh from your bones.' The baker turned as pale as flour and didn't say another word.

Three days later it was Pharaoh's birthday and he celebrated with a feast for all his servants. He got his wine steward out of prison and gave him his old job back, but he hanged the baker, just as Joseph had predicted.

Joseph sat alone in prison, listening to the distant music from Pharaoh's birthday party and hoping that the wine steward would remember his promise to put in a good word with Pharaoh. But the wine steward was so busy celebrating that he forgot all about Joseph. He didn't remember him the next day, or the day after that. In fact, he completely forgot about the talented interpreter of dreams who was gradually getting older and thinner in the dark prison under the palace. Joseph stayed there for two whole years! It looked as though his dreams of being a great man weren't going to come true – maybe no one would bow down to him after all.

To be continued…

Did Joseph ever get out of prison? Did his dreams come true? Did his family bow down before him, like the corn and the stars he dreamed about? You'll have to read on and find out in the next story: 'Cannibal cows – Pharaoh's bad dreams'.

You can read this part of Joseph's story in Genesis chapters 37, 39 and 40.

CANNIBAL COWS
Pharaoh's bad dreams

Dreadful dreams

'**AAAAAARRGH!**' yelled Pharaoh, the high king of all Egypt, as he woke up in a cold sweat in his royal bed. His heart was beating faster than a soldier's drum. He was scared stiff.

Armed guards rushed in immediately. 'What is it, your majesty?'

'**COWS!**' he yelled. 'Eating each other! **CANNIBAL COWS!** All that blood . . . and those teeth! Yuck!' He shuddered as he remembered his nightmare. 'I was on the banks of the River Nile. I looked across the water and noticed a pair of nostrils breaking the surface. At first I thought it was a crocodile, but then – guess what? – a cow came out of the river! It just rose up out of the water! It was a lovely cow, fat and well fed, and then six more exactly like it came out of the river behind it.

'I was watching them graze on the river bank when I heard a splashing behind me. I turned round and – **UGH!**' Pharaoh shuddered again and his guards looked worried. 'There were seven more cows coming out of the river, but these ones were really skinny and ugly! They were nothing but skin and bones. Then – oh, it was horrible!' Pharaoh covered his face with his hands and his guards nodded sympathetically. He took a deep breath and continued, 'The skinny cows bared their big yellow teeth and then they started eating the fat cows alive! They were **CANNIBAL COWS!** They bit off big bits of beef and licked up the blood until there was nothing left – but here's the really freaky part: they didn't get any fatter! They stayed just as skinny and ugly as before!'

Pharaoh's guards tried to reassure him that it was nothing but a silly old dream, but they left Pharaoh with his light on, just the same. Finally, he dropped off to sleep again – but it wasn't long before he was awake once more. **'AAAAARGH!'** he screamed. **'PLANTS WITH TEETH! CANNIBAL CORN!'** He told his guards what he'd dreamed this time. 'I was just looking at the crops in my fields!' he gibbered. 'I watched a tall stalk growing, with seven fat grains of wheat on it. Then, behind it, another stalk started growing, but this one was thin and weedy and it had seven skinny grains of wheat on it. Then – I'll never forget it – the skinny grains started to move towards the fat grains like hungry maggots! They opened their little mouths and ate the fat grains all up, but they still looked thin and weedy when they'd finished!'

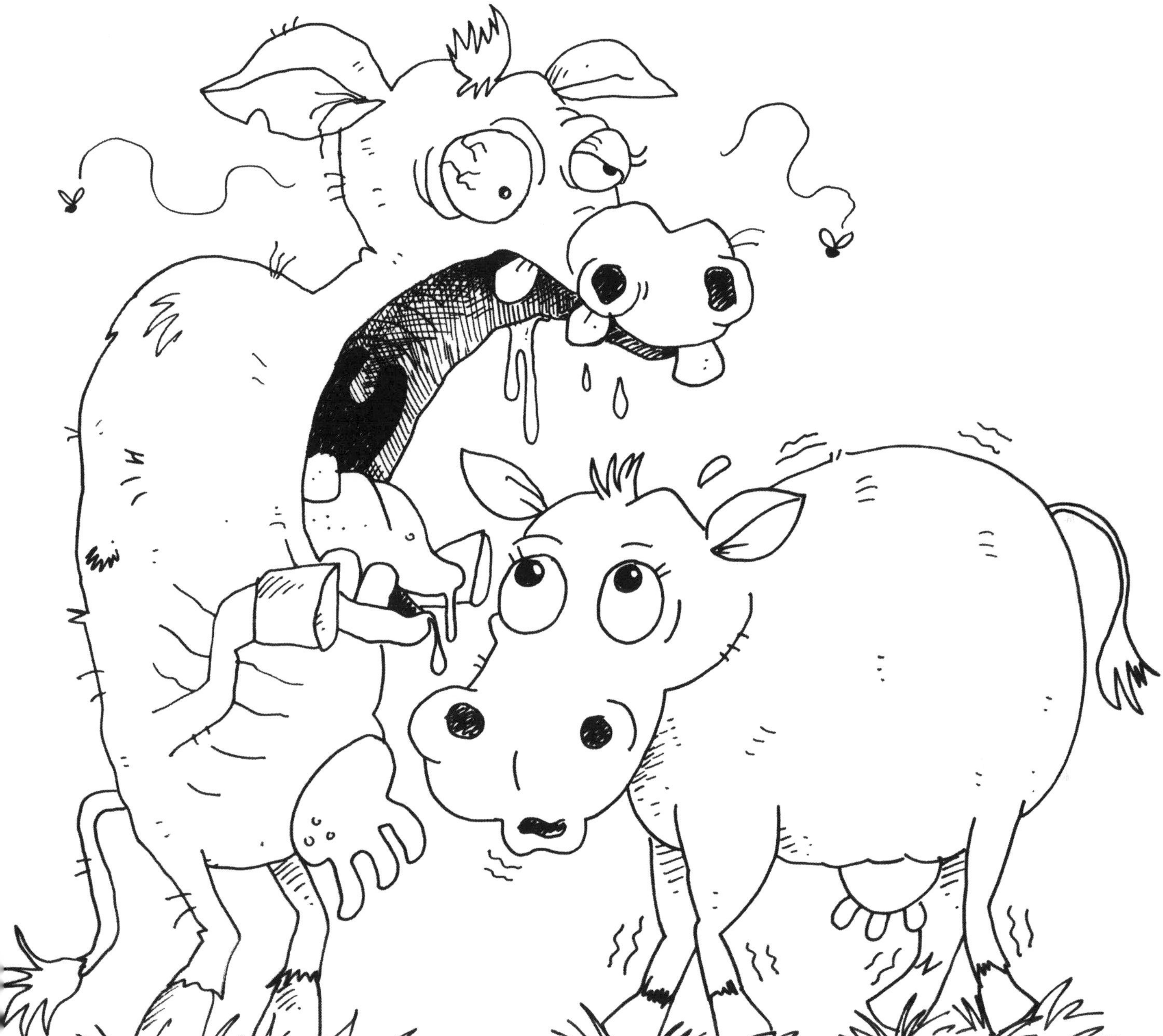

Pharaoh was a scared and shivering wreck, so his guards sent for all the wise men and wizards in Egypt to try to explain the bad dreams. Unfortunately, they all looked blank and scratched their heads. Pharaoh shouted at them, 'Can't **ANY** of you tell me what my dreams mean?'

Just at that moment, the chief wine steward arrived with a drink for Pharaoh – the very same wine steward who had been in prison with Joseph. Suddenly, two whole years after he'd promised Joseph that he wouldn't forget him and that of course he'd mention him to Pharaoh, he remembered and blurted out, 'Your majesty! I know the man you need! He's in prison and he told me and your baker what our dreams meant – and he was right!'

Pharaoh gave the order and Joseph was quickly cleaned up, given a haircut and brought to the palace. Pharaoh asked him, 'So you're the man who can interpret my dreams for me?'

'It's not me,' answered Joseph, modestly. 'God will tell you what your dreams mean.'

So Pharaoh told Joseph everything about the carnivorous cows and the cannibal corn. Joseph listened hard to Pharaoh and to God, then replied, 'These dreams both mean the same thing. They are a forecast for Egypt. The next seven years will be fantastic: you'll grow more food than ever before and everyone will be well fed. That's like the fat cows and the full grains of wheat. The seven years after that will be terrible:

all the crops will fail and your people will starve. They'll look as ill as the skinny cows.' Joseph took a deep breath as he let the bad news sink in – then he bravely told Pharaoh what to do. 'You need to put a clever man in charge to manage all the food and farming in Egypt. You need to put aside food in the good years to make sure you have enough to eat later. You need someone to organise all of this – a sensible bloke who is used to making the right decisions . . .'

Joseph waited while Pharaoh thought about this. Finally an idea occurred to Pharaoh. He pointed at Joseph. **'YOU!** What about you? You're clever and sensible and good at making the right decisions – I want **YOU** to be in charge of all the food in Egypt! What do you say?' Joseph tried to look surprised and modest, but in the end he simply said, 'Yes, please!'

Horribly hungry

So Joseph became the big boss in Egypt – no one apart from Pharaoh was more important than him. Pharaoh gave him jewels and fine clothes: at the age of 30, Joseph looked even grander than he had as a teenager, when he had worn his coloured coat and dreamed that he would become so important that even his own family would bow down to him. It looked as though his dreams were starting to come true after all.

Seven wonderful years followed. Joseph got married and had children. In Egypt, the harvests were bigger and better every year. Joseph made sure that all the spare food was safely stored away.

Sure enough, after the first seven years, the crops began to fail. The land dried up and nothing grew. It was the same all over Egypt and in the neighbouring countries. People chewed old leather to stop their tummies rumbling. Families killed stray dogs for their dinner. Children ate insects just to keep themselves alive. When the people were absolutely starving, they begged Pharaoh to help them, and he said, 'Ask Joseph.' So Joseph began to sell the grain he'd stored, and people made bread. At last the Egyptians had something to eat.

Word spread like a newsflash:

• • BREAD IN EGYPT! • •

Back in Joseph's home country, his father and brothers were starving too, so they decided to go to Egypt and buy some food. The brothers took lots of money and asked to see the man in charge. A very grand and handsome man met them: he was wearing the latest Egyptian wig and he wore fine white linen and gold jewellery. His name was even grander than he was: the Egyptians called him Zaphenathpaneah. The brothers didn't have a clue that this man was really Joseph, whom they'd sold as a slave – but Joseph recognised *them* straight away.

The brothers said, 'Please, Sir, sell us some food!' and they all bowed down to him. Joseph remembered his dream about the 11 stars and sheaves of corn that bowed to him and he smiled to himself to see his dream come true. But he hadn't finished with his brothers yet. He also remembered how they had beaten him up and bundled him into a pit, how they had left him there to rot and then sold him as a slave.

Joseph scowled at his brothers. He called them spies and liars and demanded to know all about them. When they mentioned their youngest brother, Benjamin, who was still at home with their father, Joseph's heart beat faster: Benjamin was his favourite brother – they had the same mum.

Joseph decided on a plan to test whether his brothers had changed in the years since they'd got rid of him. 'Here's the deal,' he stated. 'No more food from Egypt unless you come back with your little brother, Benjamin. Oh, and I'm keeping one of you in prison until you return.'

The brothers went back home, leaving their brother, Simeon, in an Egyptian jail, and prepared to travel straight back to Egypt. Their return journey was complicated. They took with them:

- Benjamin
- Loads of money to buy more food
- Posh presents for the Egyptian boss (they still hadn't recognised him!)

The brothers left behind:

- Their old and worried dad, Jacob
- A promise that they would look after his precious boy, Benjamin

A happy ending

Joseph met the brothers with his strictest, sternest face – but he nearly lost it when he saw his darling brother, Benjamin. He was so tearful, he hid himself in his room and cried. Then he pulled himself together: he meant to carry out his plan. He let Simeon out of jail then treated the brothers to a fantastic feast. He made sure that Benjamin was given five times as much food as anyone else. Then he loaded their sacks with the grain they'd come to buy and refused to take any money for it. Finally, he quietly ordered one of his guards to hide a precious silver cup in Benjamin's sack. He waved goodbye to his brothers as they loaded up their donkeys and set off home, happy with their success in Egypt.

When they were out of sight, he sent his guards after them with a message: 'You're thieves! One of you has stolen my precious silver cup!' After that, things happened fast.

First there was panic among the brothers: 'We haven't stolen anything!'

Next there were orders from the guards: 'You lot – back to Egypt!'

Then there was a terrible threat from Joseph: 'Whoever stole my cup will stay here forever as my slave!'

Finally there was a dreadful discovery: the cup was in Benjamin's sack. Joseph's guards grabbed the boy.

Joseph's brother, Judah, fell to his knees and begged, 'Please take me instead! This will break my father's heart! We promised him we'd look after Benjamin: the boy's mother is dead and so is his long-lost brother, Joseph. Benjamin is the only one my father has left to remind him of his favourite wife, and he'll die if anything happens to him! Make me your slave instead!'

When Joseph saw how his brothers had changed and how much they loved Benjamin and their father, he couldn't hold back his tears. He blurted out, 'It's me – your brother, Joseph!'

If you don't like sloppy scenes and happy endings, look away now . . .

Joseph hugged all his brothers, especially Benjamin. They cried until their beards were soggy with tears. Then they talked about old times and cried all over again.

Pharaoh heard the news and was really pleased for Joseph. He invited Joseph's whole family to come and live in Egypt. He said, 'You're welcome to share the best of everything!' He loaded Joseph's brothers up with treasure and new clothes, then they set off home to collect their dad and the rest of the family.

So old Jacob came to Egypt and hugged his favourite, long-lost son again. There were more tears, hugs and kisses. All Jacob's wives, children and grandchildren came too, and they were given their own land to live in, watched over by Pharaoh himself and his right-hand man, Joseph.

Both Jacob and Joseph lived good lives and died when they were very old: Jacob was 147 and Joseph was 110! God had always been on their side and he watched over their grandchildren and great-grandchildren in Egypt as they had big, strong families of their own.

So God's people settled in Egypt and the 12 families, or tribes, of Israel were named after Joseph and his brothers. As they grew, the tribes had different jobs to do: Levi's family was full of priests and Judah's tribe had lots of kings. In fact, Judah's great-great grandson was a very special king. His name was Jesus!

Egypt wasn't always a happy home for God's people. You can find out what happened to them later by reading 'Blood, bugs and boils' in **Beastly Bible Stories 4**.

You can read this part of Joseph's story in Genesis chapters 41–47.

THE SCARY STATUE AND THE CRAZY KING

Nebuchadnezzar's nightmares

Here's what had happened to God's people by the time of this story (the sixth century BC):

- First there were family arguments: God's people split up and lived separately – the kingdom of Israel in the north and the kingdom of Judah in the south.
- Then there were wars, particularly against Assyria and Babylonia.
- Finally there was disaster: the Babylonians kicked God's people out of their capital city, Jerusalem. Many of them were sent away to Babylon to work at the court of King Nebuchadnezzar.

Nasty Nebuchadnezzar

King Nebuchadnezzar was a king with a terrible temper. He was cross when his cook burned his dinner; he was furious when his fortune teller gave him bad news; he was hopping mad when his manservant lost his best slippers. Whenever King Nebuchadnezzar lost his temper, he sent for his busiest servant – his chief executioner. It was the executioner's job to drag away the cook and the fortune teller and the manservant and chop their heads off or tear their arms and legs off or kill them in whatever horrible way the king commanded.

Everyone was afraid of the king and his bad temper. However, on the night this story begins, it was the king who was afraid. He was scared to go to bed and he was terrified of going to sleep because the night before he had had a nightmare which had left him cold, sweaty and panicking. He had worried about it all day and wondered what it could mean. Now he was too frightened to turn the light off in case he had the same dream again. So at two o'clock in the morning he shouted an order: **'GUARDS! BRING ME ALL MY WIZARDS, WISE MEN, ENCHANTERS AND MAGICIANS! NOW!'**

The guards hurried to pass on the order, and all the king's wizards and wise men scurried to the king's bedroom. 'O great king! O wonderful majesty!' they grovelled. 'We are your humble servants. Tell us your dream and we will tell you what it means!'

'NO!' shouted the king. 'You'll just make something up! I'm not listening to liars! You've got to **READ MY MIND**. Here's a new law, by order of the king: if you can't tell me what my dream was and what it means, I'll rip your arms and legs off and knock your houses down!'

'But – your majesty – that's impossible!' protested the wizards and wise men. 'No one on Earth can tell what your dream was!'

'DON'T TELL ME WHAT'S IMPOSSIBLE!' shouted the king. **'EXECUTIONER! KILL THEM ALL!'** So the executioner – who was always on standby because he was the king's busiest servant – rounded up all the king's wizards, wise men, enchanters and magicians.

One of the wise men was a man of God called Daniel. He and his three friends, Shadrach, Meshach and Abednego,* had been taken from their homeland and trained at the court of King Nebuchadnezzar. They were faithful to God and God made them clever, talented and wise. He even gave Daniel the ability to interpret dreams. If there had been certificates for the best wise men in Nebuchadnezzar's court, they would have been presented to Daniel and his three friends (and their proud mums would have put them up on the wall).

The king's executioner tied up Daniel and his three friends along with all the other wise men. They watched the executioner line up lots of barrels to hold the arms and legs they were about to lose. He spread out some straw to soak up all the blood. Then Daniel shouted to the king, 'Your majesty! Give me more time and I will tell you what your dream means!'

* Their real names were Hananiah, Mishael and Azariah. The king gave them new Babylonian names – Daniel was known as Belteshazzar.

'Very well,' agreed the king, who was desperate to discover what his dream was all about. 'But this is your only chance!'

The scary statue

The executioner untied Daniel and his three friends and they rushed home. They prayed to God all day and all night. At last God showed Daniel the king's dream in a vision. 'Praise God!' shouted Daniel. 'He knows everything and now he's answered our prayers!' Daniel raced back to the executioner and said, 'Don't kill the wizards and the wise men! I'll tell the king what his dream means!'

The executioner took Daniel to the sleepless king and the king demanded, **'WELL?'**

'Well, your majesty,' began Daniel, 'your dream shows the future, and no one but God can interpret it. He has shown me your dream and told me what it means. In your dream, you were standing in the shadow of the biggest statue you had ever seen. It was huge and terrifying, like a giant, and it dazzled you. Its head was made of gold, its chest was silver, its belly and thighs were bronze, its legs were iron and its feet were made of clay with iron bones.

As you watched, a stone suddenly flew from nowhere and crashed into the statue's feet. The clay cracked, the iron creaked and then the feet crumbled. Then the whole statue toppled over: tons of gold, silver, bronze and iron came crashing

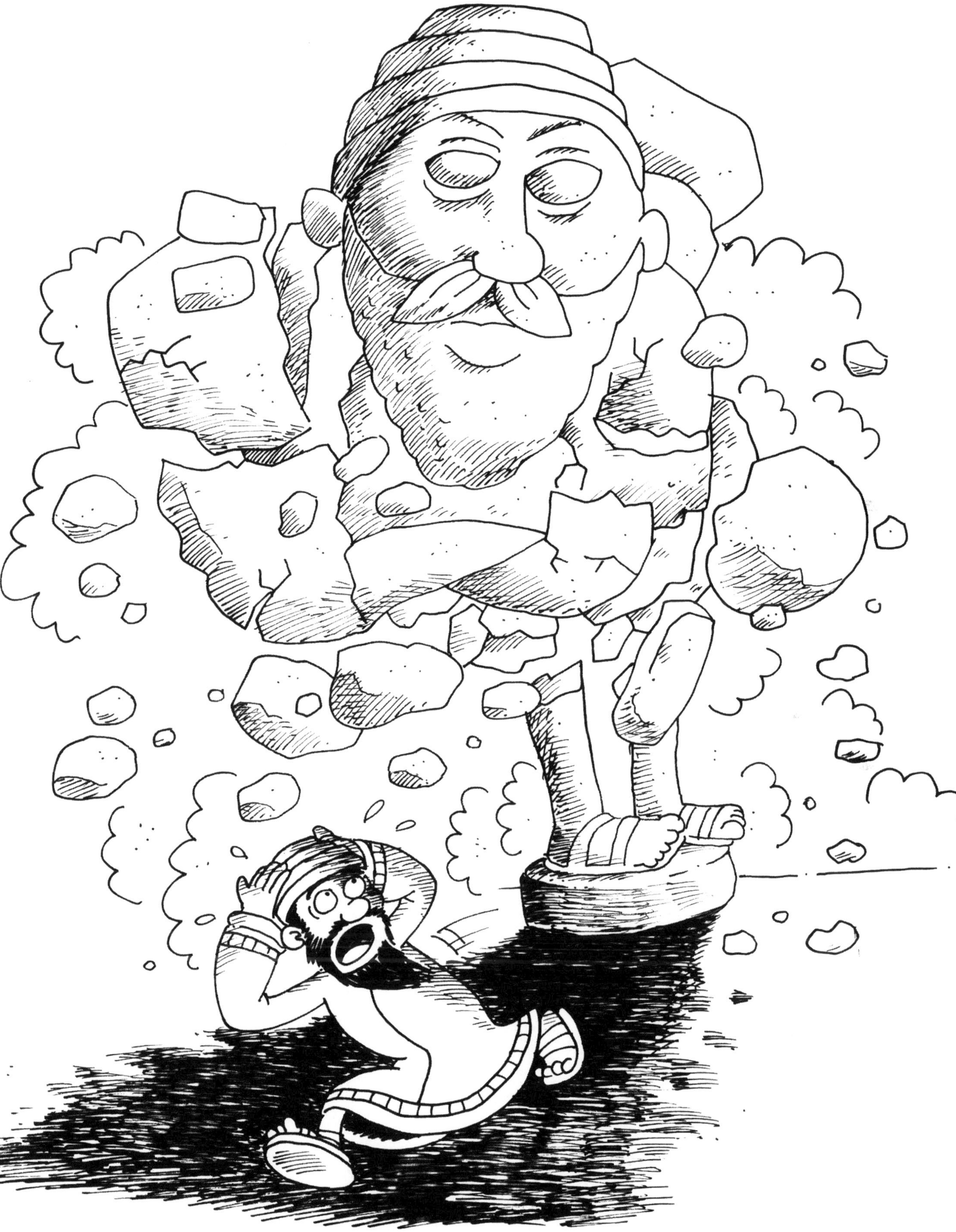

down. It all fell to bits at your feet and you watched as the rubble turned to dust which was blown away by the desert wind. But that wasn't all: the little stone that had smashed the feet started to grow in front of your eyes. It grew upwards and outwards until it became a massive mountain which filled the Earth and sky as far as you could see, and as you looked up at it you felt tinier and weaker than an ant.'

King Nebuchadnezzar said nothing. He stared at Daniel and shuddered as he remembered how frightened he had felt in his dream.

'Now, this is what your dream means,' continued Daniel. 'You, O king, are the golden head, because you are a great ruler and God has given you power over everything. After you, there will be other kingdoms. They will not be as great as yours – they are the silver and bronze bits of the statue. Then there will be a very strong kingdom – as strong as iron, which can smash anything. After that there will be a kingdom that's strong in some ways and weak in others, like the feet made of iron and clay. Finally, God will set up an everlasting kingdom which will be bigger and stronger than any other – that's like the stone that smashed the statue and grew into a massive mountain. That's God's kingdom. God has shown you the future in your dream.'

King Nebuchadnezzar fell off his throne and threw himself at Daniel's feet. 'Your God is the true God because he showed you my dream!' He was so impressed, he made Daniel the chief wise man and put him in charge of Babylon. He gave him loads of presents and promoted his friends, Shadrach, Meshach and Abednego. Daniel and his friends stayed faithful to God and, even though they still worked for King Nebuchadnezzar, life was good.

The king who became a cow

King Nebuchadnezzar had one more dreadful dream. He sent for Daniel, his chief wise man, and told him everything. 'I dreamed there was an enormous tree! It covered the whole Earth and its top branches touched heaven. It was really beautiful: animals sheltered under it, birds nested in it and everyone ate its fruit. Then I heard a voice from heaven say, "Cut down the tree! Strip off the leaves and chop off the branches! Leave the stump in the ground. As for him, he'll live with the animals. He'll wash in rainwater and I'll swap his human brain for a cow's. This will last for as long as God wants. God will show that he's the boss and he's more important than anyone." So who was the dream talking about? What does it all mean?' asked Nebuchadnezzar nervously.

Daniel gulped. He wouldn't wish a dream like that on his worst enemy. What would the king say when he told him what it meant?

'What's wrong? Don't be frightened – just tell me!' pleaded the king when he saw the look on Daniel's face.

'Well,' began Daniel, 'the great tree is you, O great king! You're strong and everyone looks up to you. But I'm afraid God is going to destroy you – he's going to send you away to live like an animal! But in your dream the tree stump was left – that means your kingdom will grow again, once you've learned that God is in charge. I'm really sorry.'

A year later, the king was walking on the roof of his palace in Babylon and he admired his beautiful city spread out before him. 'Just look at that!' he said out loud. 'Look what a magnificent city I've built! I'm the one with all the power and the glory round here!'

Before he could say another word, a voice from heaven shouted, 'GOD's the one with the power and the glory, and he's going to teach you a lesson!'

Then Nebuchadnezzar ran screaming out of the city and went completely bonkers. First he took off all his clothes. Then he walked around on all fours. After a while he shared a field with some cows and learned how to moo. When he was hungry he ate grass (don't try this at home), and when he needed a bath he let the rain wash over his back. He lived wild for so long that the cows got used to him and kept him warm at night. His hair grew into a shaggy coat and his nails grew long, curved and yellow, like an eagle's claws.

One day, quite suddenly, Nebuchadnezzar's mind cleared, and the first words he said were, 'God is in charge! Power and glory are his for ever!' He had learned his lesson.

He made his way back to his palace where he was welcomed home. He washed the cow dung off his feet, cut his claws and shaved off his shaggy mane. His servants brought him fine clothes and jewels, then he sat down on his throne and put his crown back on his head. 'That's better!' he sighed.

From that day on, Nebuchadnezzar's kingdom grew even more powerful. He knew that God was in charge, because everything had happened just as his dreadful dream – and Daniel – had said it would.

Daniel and his friends had more dramatic adventures in Babylon: you can read about how they faced hungry lions and a fiery furnace in 'Eaten alive' and 'Burned alive' in **Beastly Bible Stories 4***.*

You can read about these dreams in Daniel chapters 1, 2 and 4.

RIGHT AND WRONG

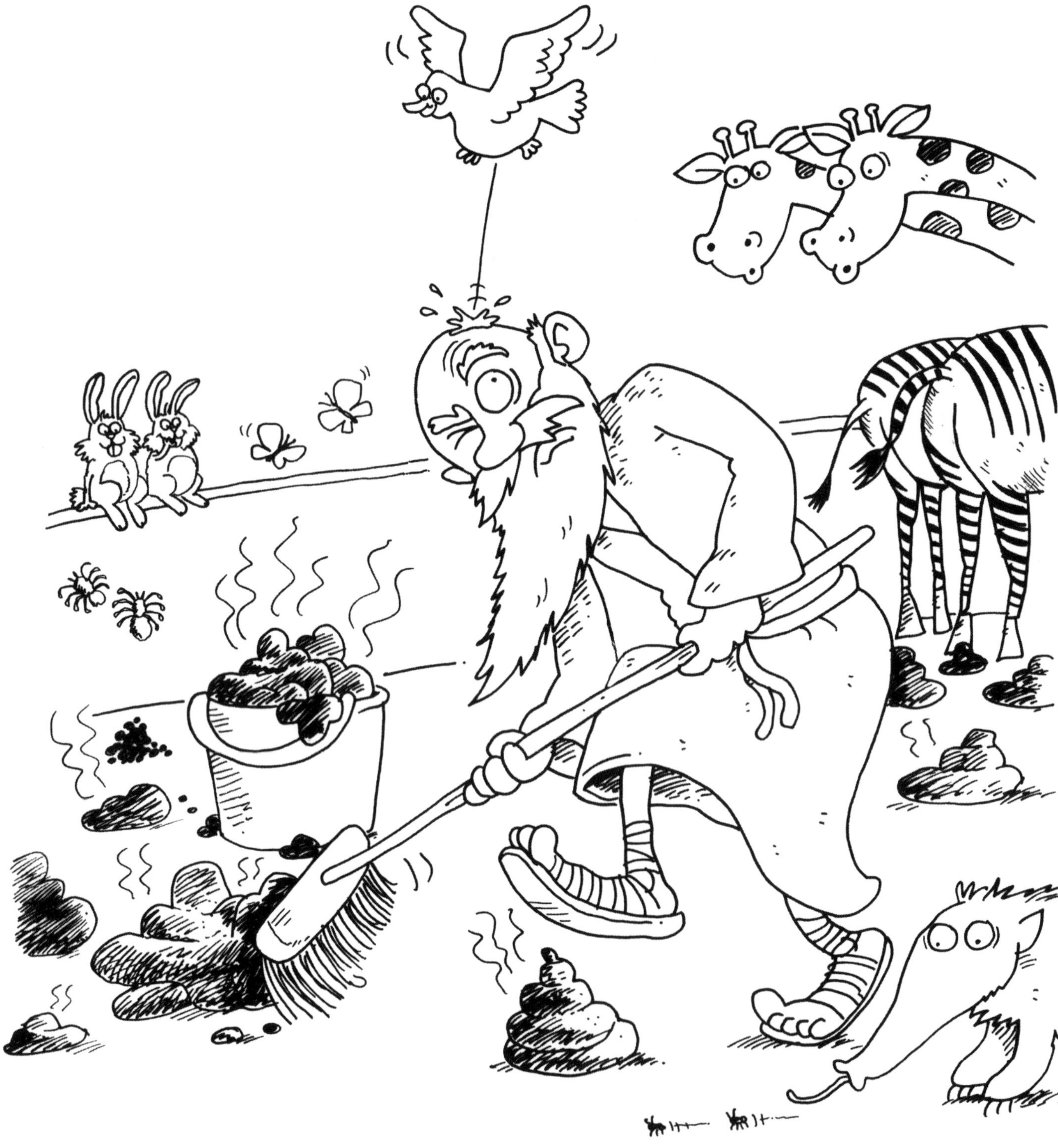

THE FATAL FLOOD
Noah and the ark

A terrible stink

'THERE'S POO EVERYWHERE!' shouted Noah. 'WHOSE TURN IS IT TO MUCK OUT?' Noah looked across the deck of the big boat he'd built with his own hands. Wherever he walked, he squelched in muck, manure, dung and droppings. 'It's time to clear this lot up – again!'

Noah's sons sighed and reached for their shovels. They'd had 40 days of this. They were adrift on an endless sea and they were cooped up in their father's floating zoo with pairs of every kind of animal – birds, mammals, reptiles and insects. Every kind of animal meant every kind of animal poo. Each morning they shovelled tons of the stuff overboard, and each evening there was more. The stink was terrible! Even passing sharks wished they could hold their noses.

The fatal flood

The floating zoo and the endless sea were all part of God's plan to clean up his creation. He'd made the world and it was good, but then it had all gone bad because people had forgotten the difference between right and wrong. They fought and killed each other; they were selfish and cruel. So God decided to scrap them all and start again. The world as he'd made it would be wiped out. There was only one person God wanted to save: a good and faithful man called Noah.

God told Noah exactly what to do. He gave him the plans for a big boat which he called an ark. He gave him all the measurements and detailed carpentry instructions. As for the crew, God told Noah to take his entire family, including his sons and their wives. Finally God gave Noah a little list and a big job:

Ark cargo
1. **One pair of every kind of animal (plus extra pairs of clean animals*)**
2. **The right food for everyone**

What a job! It took Noah a long time to load up the ark. The cats kept eating the mice, the rabbits kept making babies, the fleas kept finding new homes and Noah lost count of the ants. The vultures and the jackals fought over their food and the pandas sulked because they didn't like each other.

At last Noah was ready. The crew and the cargo were on board and God himself closed the door behind them. Then it started to rain. This was all part of God's plan: he wanted to wash the Earth clean with an enormous flood. Here's Noah's record of what happened (like all good captains, he kept a diary in his ship's log).

---

* In Jewish law, animals and birds are either clean or unclean (see *Clean and unclean – rules for eating* later in this book.) You'll find out at the end of this story why Noah needed the extra pairs...

SHIP'S LOG

Day 1

Rain started falling just after breakfast. The sky is covered with thick grey clouds. Heavy rain has been hammering on the roof of the ark all day. It's very noisy on board, what with the rain and the roaring, trumpeting, squeaking, barking, mooing, etc. None of the animals likes being cooped up, and to be honest, neither do I. However, my job is to follow God's orders.

Day 2

It has been raining all night. The river has burst its banks but the ark is still on dry land. The animals are getting restless.

Day 3

Still raining. Brown flood water is rushing through all the valleys round here. Whole trees have floated by. Monkeys keep trying to climb onto the ark, but they're not allowed in – we've got enough monkeys, and God gave strict orders about numbers.

Day 4

The water is still rising. Homes have been flooded and I've seen people floating past, clinging to bits of furniture. They shouted to us to rescue them. I feel bad about leaving them behind, but we're fully loaded. God has shut us all in and I don't have the key to the ark's front door.

Day 5

The ark is afloat! Water everywhere. Animals and crew now being seasick. Need more buckets.

Day 6

Still raining. I can only see treetops now. We are all trying to ignore the floating dead bodies outside — cows, sheep, cats, dogs and lots of people. The flood has drowned everything and everybody, apart from us. Even if it is part of God's plan, it's still very sad.

Days 7-12

Still raining. Noisy and smelly on board. Animals and people complaining.

Day 13

Still raining. Now I can't even see the mountain tops any more. There's just this ark, floating on an endless sea under a stormy sky. I wish I'd packed more fresh fruit – I really fancy an orange now.

Day 14

Still raining . . .

After this, the ship's log gets rather boring, because it rained for 40 days and 40 nights! At last, on Day 41, something new happened.

Day 41

IT HAS STOPPED RAINING! WE CAN SEE BLUE SKY! We have been celebrating all day. I sent one of the ravens out to explore, but it still hasn't come back. Maybe all the trees are still underwater.

Noah waited for the raven to come back, but it never did. It just kept flying over the water, desperately looking for a place to land. Later on, he sent out a dove, but she just flew around for a while and came straight back to the ark. Later still, Noah sent out another dove. By this time, everyone was impatient to see some sign that the flood waters were draining away. Was there any dry land out there at all?

Day 143

GREAT NEWS! My dove has come back with a fresh olive leaf in her beak! Somewhere there must be dry land! Trees are starting to grow again! Soon we'll be getting off this ark! God hasn't given up on us, after all! HOORAY! We're still afloat for now, although mountain tops are starting to poke out of the sea like tiny desert islands.

Day 150

LAND AHOY! The ark has run aground! I think we're on top of a mountain — we'll see. The water level is still dropping. Heaven knows where we are!

Freedom and fresh meat

Noah's ark had run aground on top of a mountain called Ararat. Day by day, very slowly, the flood waters drained away like a giant's bath water until at last the land was dry. Finally, God let everyone out of the ark. Noah's family left first, and they were nearly trampled by the stampede that followed. The animals couldn't wait to escape! You know how you feel at the end of a long car journey — and the animals on the ark didn't even have music or DVDs to keep them entertained. Over-excited emus, travel-sick tapirs and bored badgers all charged out of the ark, free at last.

'Get busy!' God told everyone. 'Make yourselves at home and make babies!' Everyone liked the sound of that. However, Noah had something else that he needed to do first. He built a stone altar and cut down a young tree for firewood. Then he sharpened his great big knife (the one he used for cutting up meat). After that he rounded up all the clean animals, who were busy enjoying the first fresh grass they'd tasted for months, and all the clean birds, who were building new nests. He chose one of each* – then killed the lot! He was very grateful that God had saved them all so he made a massive animal sacrifice to say thank you: he piled all the dead bodies on the altar and burned them.

God smelled the delicious barbecue smell of roasting cow and toasting chicken. He smiled and said to himself, 'I'll never destroy the Earth again.' Then he said to Noah, 'Have a huge family! Human beings are in charge – you'll be the boss of everything and all these animals will be afraid of you. They'll be your food, but you mustn't eat their blood. Now – go and make babies!'

Finally God made a promise – a pact – with Noah and his family. He said, 'I'll never destroy the Earth again. You're all my living creatures and we're on the same side, you and I. Here's the sign that I'll never break my promise.' With that, God did something wonderful with sunlight and raindrops and created a

---

* For the Jews, only clean animals may be eaten or sacrificed. Noah's lions, wolves, pigs and rats were all unclean, so they were safe, and so were the eagles, vultures and seagulls. But cows and sheep were on the menu, and chickens were for the chop. Now you know why Noah took extra pairs of clean animals onto the ark!

rainbow that spread its multicoloured arch across the sky. 'There!' said God. 'This rainbow will remind us of our pact.'

And so creation got off to a fresh start. Noah lived to see his family grow and grow, just as God had wanted. He must have seen a lot of grandchildren because the Bible says that Noah died when he was 950 years old!

God's promise to Noah is important because the whole Bible is the story of God's pact with humankind. It tells us how God chose his special people and what happened when they didn't keep their part of the deal (God was always on their side, but they weren't always on his). As you read more **Beastly Bible Stories,** *look out for the ways in which God renewed and kept his promise to love his people.*

You can read the story of Noah in Genesis chapters 6–9.

BABBLING BUILDERS
The Tower of Babel

Big plans

'OOOOOOH!' When the red cloth was whipped away, the people were impressed by what they saw. Those who were at the back of the crowd shoved forwards for a better view. They craned their necks to see important men on a platform pointing proudly at the large shiny model they had just unveiled. It was a scale model of massive buildings, tall towers, wide streets and mighty walls – the building plan for a great city. In the centre was a huge temple, like a pyramid with a tower on top. Hundreds of steps led all the way up to the top of the tower, which would be tall enough to get lost in the clouds. Everyone clapped when they saw how wonderful their new city would look.

'Now listen – here's the plan,' said one of the men in charge. Everyone listened hard. 'We'll all work together to build this. The world has never seen anything like it! With all the talented artists, great builders and hard workers we have among us, **ANYTHING's** possible. What do you say – shall we build this city?'

The crowd roared its answer with one voice: **'YES!'** No one complained, no one argued and no one said, 'How much is this going to cost us?' because in those days, the world was very young and the human race was like one big, happy family. The people all spoke the same language and they understood each other perfectly. Working together was easy.

'Just you wait – we'll be famous!' continued the man in charge. 'We'll really make a name for ourselves! We'll settle here and be the biggest and best city in the world! Our tower will be so high, we'll be able to see eye to eye with God himself!' Everyone cheered wildly.

God was listening in and he didn't like the sound of that. He decided to keep a close eye on these people and their building project.

So the people organised themselves into teams and worked round the clock to make millions of bricks for their city and its great tower. Next they worked together to build the foundations and even took it in turns to share each other's tools. (Never in the history of the world has there been such good group work – your teacher would have been impressed.) Then, brick by brick, they began to build the walls and raise up the tower. As the tower stretched into the sky, the people felt proud of themselves. 'Look at what we can do!' they said to each other. 'We're really something special, you know. If we can build this, then **ANYTHING's** possible!'

God looked at the tower that was pointing up to heaven like a finger. When he heard how proud the people were, it confirmed his worst fears. They were wrong to be so big-headed. 'Look at them,' he said to himself. 'They're like one big, happy family and they all speak the same language. But they're getting too big for their boots. This city is just the beginning – if they can build this, then **ANYTHING's** possible! I can't have that! I'm going to make things a bit harder for them. I'm going to mix up their language, then they won't understand each other so easily.'

The punch-up

So God went down to the city and confused the people's language. He scrambled the sounds and mixed up the names for things. Brick-makers were busy making bricks and builders were busy building so no one realised anything had happened until one builder shouted, 'Pass me that trowel!'

His mate replied, 'Qué?' which means 'What?' in Spanish.

Then the baffled builder turned to his neighbour to ask what was wrong, and his neighbour answered, 'Was?' which means 'What?' in German.

The man in charge asked why the builders had stopped work, and the foreman answered, 'Mujhey nahi maloom!' which means 'I don't know!' in Hindi. Then the builder who wanted the trowel snatched it anyway and the man who owned it tried to grab it back – and that's how the fight started. The builders gave up on words and used their fists instead: **OOF! WOMPF! CRUCK! DOOF!**

Meanwhile, the builders' wives were trying to buy food in the marketplace. 'Bikam?' said one, which means 'How much?' in Arabic.

'Quid dicis?' replied the man who ran the market stall, which means 'What are you saying?' in Latin.

An impatient women in the long queue shouted crossly, 'Qu'est-ce que c'est?' which means 'What is it?' in French.

The woman behind her snapped, 'Pose leg-ace?' which means 'What are you saying?' in Greek – and that's how the argument started. People shouted insults in many different languages. Friends turned on each other and yelled in frustration. Some people simply gave up talking and made signs with their hands that were easier to understand but rather rude.

The city was in chaos! In every street and square there was a huge shouty noise – a confused babble of different languages. At the end of the morning, the builders walked away from their work. At the end of the day, many people went off in a huff to find someone they could understand. Some stayed in a silent sulk. At the end of the week, whole families decided to leave the city for good and live somewhere else instead.

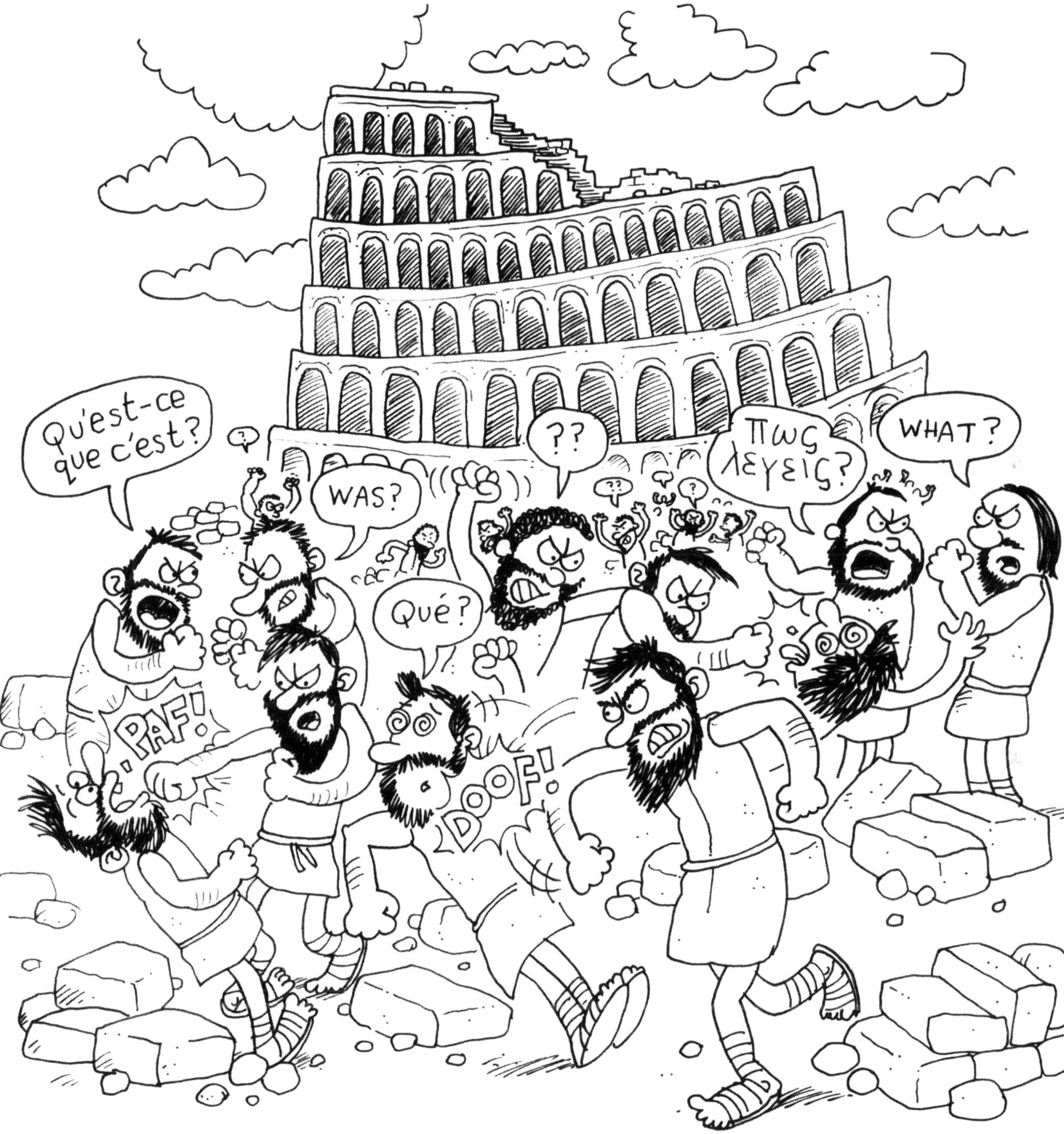
Qu'est-ce que c'est?
WAS?
Qué?
??
Πως λεγεις?
WHAT?
PAF!
DOOF!

So gradually, over weeks and months and years and generations, people learned to stick with others who spoke like them; in their different family groups they began to spread out all over the world. God watched them go.

The unfinished city

Dust gathered on the shiny model of the great city that never was, because no one bothered to look at the plans any more. Birds nested in the roofless palaces. The city walls were never finished. The tall tower – the people's pride and joy – only reached halfway to heaven. It pointed limply at God like a broken finger. People used the bricks for their own houses and built their own walls to keep the neighbours out. The unfinished city was called Babel, because everyone remembered the confused babble of different languages there.

God had put the people in their place. He'd scrambled their speech into different languages and spread them all over the world, which is the situation we find ourselves in today.

This story reminds us that God is in charge and that he decides who will have a great future – the people of Babel were wrong to decide that for themselves. Much later, Babel became the great city of Babylon, the capital city of Israel's powerful enemies, the Babylonians. The story of Babel also shows that for people who understand each other, ANYTHING's possible! Remember this when you read what God did with different languages on the day of Pentecost in 'Wind, wildfire and wonderful words' in **Beastly Bible Stories – The Terrific New Testament**.

You can read the story of the Tower of Babel in Genesis chapter 11.

THE CRUCIAL CUT

The circumcision rule

The unbreakable promise

'**ABRAM!**' said a kind voice. Abram woke up from his mid-afternoon doze. He was an old man of 99, after all. He was also a good and faithful man who had always done things God's way. He looked up at the stranger in front of him – a stranger who seemed to shine and shimmer like the desert sun.

'Who are you?' whispered Abram.

'I am **GOD** Almighty!' the stranger announced, and Abram knew it was true. He threw himself down at God's feet.

'Here's the deal,' said God. 'You and I are going to make a pact.* Here's what I'll do for you: first, I'm going to give you a huge family and millions of descendants. You'll be the father of kings and whole nations. Second, I'm giving you a new name: Abraham. It means 'father of many.' Third, I'll make a pact with you and all your family and descendants. I'll be your God and you'll be my special people – that's an everlasting promise. Finally, I'll give you the land of Canaan as your homeland.'

* The Bible calls this unbreakable promise a covenant.

What a promise! Abraham knew he'd give his right arm to have everything that God offered – but it wasn't his right arm that God wanted. Abraham was going to have to cut off something else (if you're squeamish, look away now).

God continued, 'Now you must seal this pact between us. I want you and all your sons and all the men in your house to be circumcised.'

Beastly Bible fact

Circumcision means 'cutting around'. It's a big word for a little operation in which the flap of skin (or foreskin) at the end of a boy's penis is cut off. It's called being circumcised.

Abraham sat up straight, crossed his legs and gulped. God explained, 'You've got to do this to show that you belong to me and that you're keeping your part of the pact we've made. Seal the deal with your skin.'

While Abraham thought about this, God went into more detail about his promises: 'I'm giving your wife, Sarai, a new name: Sarah. It means Princess. Sarah will have a son – she'll be the mother of kings and whole nations.'

When he heard this, Abraham fell on the floor again, but this time he was laughing, not bowing. **'HA HA HA!'** He held his sides and laughed until he cried. 'Good one, Lord!' he gasped. 'I'll be 100 next year, and Sarah will be 90! Imagine – us having a baby! That's a laugh!'

God didn't laugh. He waited patiently for Abraham to get his breath back.

Eventually Abraham said, 'Look, God, I've had one son – Ishmael – with my wife's slave. Bless him instead!'

God replied, 'No. Sarah **WILL** have a son and you'll call him Isaac. I'll make a pact with him and all his family and descendants. I won't forget Ishmael, though – his 12 sons will be princes, and I'll make him the father of a great nation, too. But Isaac's family will be my special people and I will be their God.'

With that, God left. Abraham went straight home and sharpened his best knife. He was 99 and his son Ishmael was 13. They were both circumcised that day, along with all the men in the household, including the servants and slaves.

Ever since Abraham's circumcision sealed his pact with God, Jewish baby boys have been circumcised. Nowadays the operation is usually done in hospital under anaesthetic and the baby doesn't remember it, but things were different in the days of these Bible stories. There were no painkillers, for a start, and it was often grown-up men who were circumcised. Circumcision in the Bible happened for a number of reasons – not all of them good…

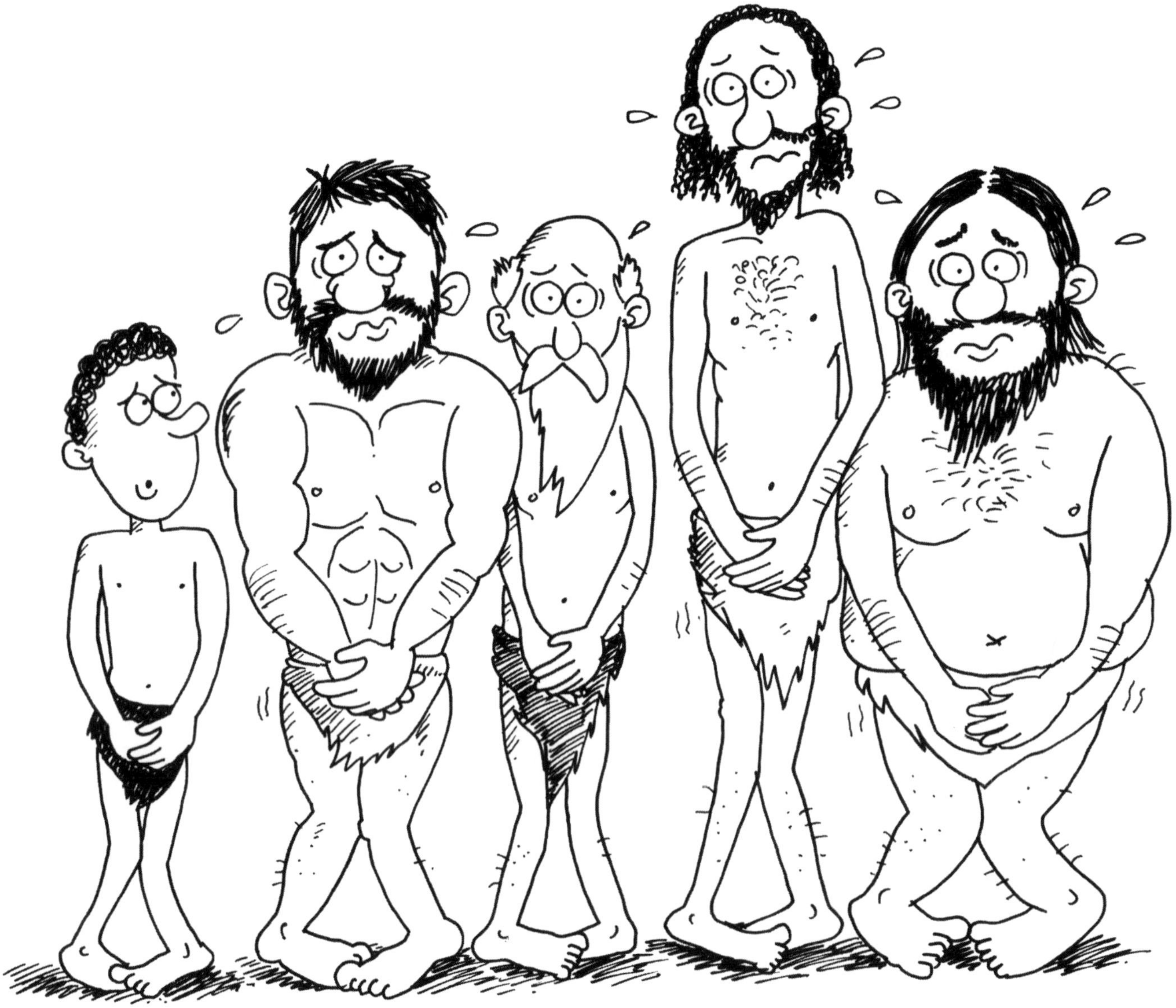

A weapon of war

A foreigner called Shechem attacked a Jewish girl called Dinah, then said he wanted to marry her. Dinah's brothers plotted revenge. They told Shechem that he and all the men in his house had to be circumcised before the wedding if they were going to become part of their family. Three days after the circumcision, when Shechem and all his men were still in pain and wearing bandages instead of pants, Dinah's brothers attacked and killed them all!

A special sign

The Jews got out of the habit of circumcising their baby boys during the 40 years they spent in the wilderness.* Before God let them settle in the land he'd promised them, he told all the men to be circumcised. They made knives out of sharp flint and did as they were told. **(OUCH!)** This was a fresh start for God's people – a sign that the pact between them and God was as strong as ever.

A deadly dowry

When David** wanted to marry the daughter of King Saul, Saul plotted to get rid of him. This was his plan: to demand a dowry (a bride's price) that would lead to David's certain death. So he didn't ask for gold or treasure in exchange for his

---

* You can discover why they ended up in the wilderness in *Blood, bugs and boils* in **Beastly Bible Stories 4**.
** You can read his story in *The giant killer* in **Beastly Bible Stories 1**.

daughter; he asked for 100 Philistine foreskins! This meant that David would have to circumcise 100 of his people's deadliest enemies. Of course, the Philistines wouldn't be keen on this idea, so David would have to fight them first. Saul reckoned this would be the end of David, but David and his men triumphed over their enemies. They brought back double the dowry – 200 Philistine foreskins!

Since Abraham was circumcised, it has been traditional for his male descendants to be circumcised too. It's seen as a special sign of belonging to God. Most Christians don't do circumcision – instead, baptism is the Christian sign of following Jesus.

Abraham and his sons had other adventures. You can find out what happened in 'The banished brother' and 'The human sacrifice' in **Beastly Bible Stories 3**.

You can read these circumcision stories in Genesis chapters 17 and 34, Joshua chapter 5 and 1 Samuel chapter 18.

SIN CITIES
Sodom and Gomorrah

Crime and punishment

Have you heard of the Dead Sea? It's a sea so salty that nothing can live in it. It's surrounded by desert, and on its beaches the salt piles up into strange shapes. There are blocks of salt as big as boulders, towers of salt like giant toadstools and pillars of salt the size of people. When the tourists go home, the pillars of salt watch silently over the Dead Sea.

If you could travel thousands of years back in time, the place would look rather different. Imagine – instead of dry rocks there are green fields, and instead of desert there are two big, busy, noisy, smelly cities. Instead of pillars of salt there are thousands of people. Come closer and you'll see what the people are doing in the city streets. Look! There are two women fighting over a baby. Look! There's a gang of children stealing an old man's dinner. Look! There's an angry mob of men with knives who are about to – on second thoughts, look away. You're in the city of Sodom and I'd leave NOW if I were you – and I wouldn't go next door to Gomorrah, either. Sodom and Gomorrah are the notorious cities of sin, wickedness and general bad behaviour. If you must visit, don't go there alone – or after dark.

God had been receiving lots of complaints about Sodom and Gomorrah. He wanted to take a closer look – were they as bad as people said? If the cities were rotten from top to bottom, God planned to punish them. No more warnings – he'd wipe them out. But first he decided to talk his plans through with Abraham (they were very close – do you remember the special pact that God made with Abraham in the last story?). God wanted Abraham and his family to be clear about the difference between right and wrong, and to understand that he – God – was a fair judge.

So God sent two angels to Sodom to investigate while he talked to Abraham. Abraham was horrified by the threat of God's punishment. 'But Lord, will you really wipe out two whole cities? I know they're wicked, but what if there are some good people there?'

God had already thought of this and he was secretly pleased that Abraham had asked.

'Well, OK – if I find 50 good people there, I'll let everyone off the hook. They'll all be forgiven.' God knew that he'd do the same for the sake of just ten good people among thousands of wicked ones, but he let Abraham carry on asking.

'I'm sorry, Lord, I don't mean to tell you what to do – but what if there are only 45 good people? I have to ask – what if there are only 40? Or 30? Or 20? Forgive me for being so pushy – you made me, after all – but what if you only find ten good people in those cities?'

God smiled and reassured Abraham. 'Even if my angels only find ten good people there, I'll forgive everyone.' Abraham thought of his nephew, Lot, and his family who lived in Sodom. He hoped that they were good enough.

An angry mob

In Sodom, it was getting late. Abraham's nephew, Lot, was keeping a lookout for any trouble before he locked his doors and barred his windows for the night. He watched as two grand strangers arrived at the city gates and he saw all the local thugs and thieves eyeing up their fine clothes. Those bored, bad men were clearly looking forward to spilling some blood – they watched the new arrivals like wolves stalking a pair of lambs. Lot acted quickly and bowed to the men. 'Please, my lords, let me offer you a bed for the night.'

'Thank you,' replied the strangers, 'but we'll be fine camping out here in the town square.' (Being angels, they were a trusting pair and not very streetwise – Sodom was not at all like heaven.)

Lot could see the thugs gathering into a gang around the two strangers and he said, 'Seriously, that's not a good idea. Come with me – quickly!' The mob started muttering and the strangers decided that bed and breakfast at Lot's house sounded like a better plan, after all.

Once all three were safely inside and the front door was locked and bolted, Lot welcomed the strangers to join his family for dinner. Lot's wife washed the guests' feet and his grown-up daughters baked fresh bread. They laid a feast in front of their guests, who shared the food and drink gratefully.

By the time they had eaten, it was nearly midnight. Lot's daughters were making up beds for the unexpected visitors and Lot's wife was blowing out the lamps around the house when there was a loud, rude hammering at the front door, followed by shouting and swearing. Terrified, Lot peered out of an upstairs window and saw a huge gang of men surrounding his house – it was an even bigger, angrier mob than before. Every man and boy in the city seemed to be there! They bellowed their questions and answers at Lot:

'WHAT DO WE WANT?'
'YOUR TWO VISITORS!'
'WHEN DO WE WANT THEM?'
'NOW!'
'WHAT WILL WE DO TO THEM?'

The answers were too rude to repeat here, but the mob cheered viciously. Lot bravely stepped outside his front door to face them. 'Come on guys, have a heart,' he pleaded. 'I'd give you my own daughters before I'd hand over these two men to you. They're my guests – please show some respect!'

'WHO ARE YOU TO TELL US WHAT TO DO?' yelled a thug with big muscles and ugly tattoos. 'COME ON, LADS – LET'S GET HIM!' The crowd roared and surged forward to grab Lot. Just in the nick of time, Lot's guests pulled open the front door and dragged him inside.

Fire and brimstone

Lot and his guests leant heavily against the door as they listened to the angry mob stamping closer and closer. Suddenly the two guests yelled, **'NOW!'**

Outside the door there was a flash of bright light, followed by a panicky cry from the crowd: **'AAARGH!'** Lot heard thumps and yells, but now the mob sounded more scared than angry. He peeped through a crack in the wall and saw the men stumbling about, clutching their eyes. They had all gone blind! They couldn't see Lot or his guests – they couldn't even find his front door!

Lot gawped at his guests. What had they done? He had never seen such power – what kind of men were they? The two angels turned to Lot. 'We are going to destroy this place. The wicked people of Sodom and Gomorrah have seriously offended God, so he has sent us to wipe them from the face of the earth. You will escape if you and your family get out **NOW!'**

Lot rounded up his family and ran to tell the men who were going to marry his daughters – 'God's going to wipe this place out! We've got to get out NOW!' But the men were half asleep and thought Lot was joking.

By the time the sun came up, the angels were ready to strike, but Lot still hadn't left the city. His donkey was loaded up and his wife was ready, but his daughters were crying and refusing to leave without their husbands-to-be. Finally the angels lost patience with them all – they grabbed the family and half-dragged, half-carried them to the city gates. 'Now run for your lives!' they shouted. 'Head for the hills or you'll die too! Don't stop for anything and, whatever you do, **DON'T LOOK BACK!'**

'But,' said Lot, 'the hills are miles away! We'll never make it! The city of Zoar is nearer – can't we go there?'

The angels sighed impatiently. **'OK, OK,** go to Zoar, but get a move on! We can't get started here until you're out of the way!'

Lot and his wife and his two daughters headed away from the city, panicked by the look of deadly purpose in the angels' eyes. God watched them go. Then he turned to the sinful cities of Sodom and Gomorrah and gave the order. **CCCRRRAAAAAAAACKK!** The earth shook and split open and a great fountain of fire and lava spewed into the air. It looked like the end of the world! Flaming lumps of rock and sulphur* rained down on the cities and set

* The Bible calls this 'fire and brimstone'.

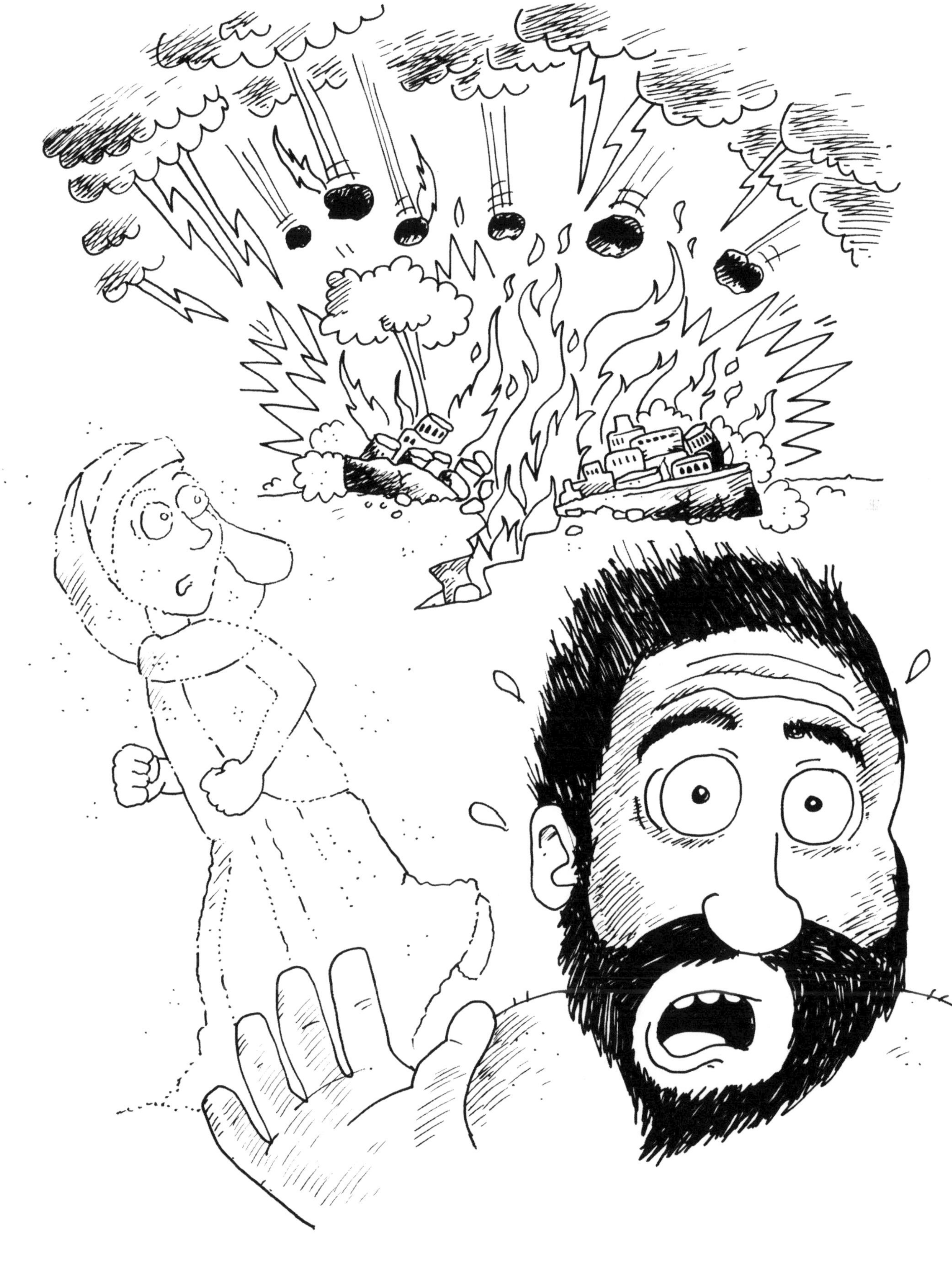

fire to everything; whole buildings disappeared into gaping holes in the ground. The rumbling and the roaring and the hissing and the exploding drowned the noise of thousands of people screaming.

Pass the salt

Out in the desert, Lot and his family hurried on towards Zoar and safety. Only his wife looked back to see her city, her home and her friends turning to dust and ashes. Her husband and daughters walked on ahead, but she lingered so long that a wave of hot rock and ash overtook her – she was cooked inside a crust of mega-hot minerals. When Lot reached the outskirts of Zoar at last, he turned to call his daughters and they came – but where was his wife? He could see nothing but a sky filled with black smoke, the smouldering remains of Sodom and Gomorrah and a pillar of salt, which was exactly his wife's height, standing in the distance on the smoking ground.

Today, the Dead Sea covers the flatlands where perhaps Sodom and Gomorrah once stood. The burnt fields turned to desert and nothing can live in the salty sea. Pillars of salt still stand, like Lot's wife, gazing blankly over the lifeless plain.

The story of Sodom and Gomorrah is a warning that God takes right and wrong seriously – but he is a kind and fair judge who wanted to know the truth before he handed out punishment, and who would have spared both cities for the sake of just ten good people, although in the end only Lot and his family were saved. As for Lot's wife – perhaps she didn't really want to leave Sodom, and that's why she looked back. Unfortunately, she paid the same price as the people who had stayed behind.

You can read this story in Genesis chapters 18 and 19.

LAWS FOR LIVING
The Ten Commandments

Mind-blowing mountain mayhem

BRRRRRRRROOAARGH! The thunder roared from the black clouds like a lion with toothache.

CRAAACKCKCK! Lightning split the dark sky – the white-hot bolt sizzled as it hit the ground.

PAAAAAAAAAARP! The deafening blast of a heavenly trumpet sounded louder than a low-flying jet.

God's special people, the Israelites, were standing in the desert in the shadow of the mighty Mount Sinai, clutching their ears and shaking with fear as the storm raged above them. The man in charge was called Moses* – he had been chosen by God to lead the Israelites, and he'd just told them all to smarten themselves up, be on their best behaviour and gather in front of the mountain to meet their God. He'd also warned them not to touch the mountain or they'd die. **(GULP.)**

---

* You can find out why Moses and the Israelites were in the desert in the first place by reading *Blood, bugs and boils*, *Blood on the door* and *Walking under the waves* in **Beastly Bible Stories 4**.

As the people stood carefully not touching the rocky slopes of the mountain, God arrived on the mountain top in a whirl of wildfire and the summit was smothered in thick, black smoke. The mountain started to shake and shiver as if it were terrified. God's people knew how it felt.

PAAAAAAAAARP! PAAAAAAAAARP! The heavenly trumpet sounded even more loudly and above the blast Moses yelled, **'LORD, WE'RE HERE!'**

'BRRRRRRRRYOUAAAARERRGHHERERRRRR!' replied God in the thunder.

Then Moses began to climb the mountain. The people gasped as he disappeared into the thundering cloud that was full of smoke, fire and lightning. Would they ever see him again?

Then God's voice boomed out of the cloud. It was louder than the thunder's rumble, clearer than the lightning's crackle and more powerful than the trumpet's blast. Every single one of God's people heard what he said:

'Rule number one:
I AM YOUR GOD – only me; no one else.

Rule number two:
don't worship statues or idols or anything else
that you've made yourselves.

Rule number three:
say my name with respect.

Rule number four:
have a day off on the Sabbath – it's my holy day.*

Rule number five:
honour your parents.

Rule number six:
do not kill.

Rule number seven:
be faithful in marriage.

Rule number eight:
do not steal.

Rule number nine:
don't tell lies.

Rule number ten:
don't long for things that belong to someone else.'

* The Sabbath is the seventh day of the week – Saturday for Jews, Sunday for Christians.

God gave his people many other laws, rules and instructions, but these first ten were the biggies. These were the laws for living that have become known as the Ten Commandments. God gave them to his people to show them how to live good, happy lives: all the Israelites had to do was live by the rules. What could possibly go wrong?

A bloodbath seals the deal

The Israelites huddled together at the foot of the mountain under the smoke and the storm. They were absolutely terrified of God's power. They shouted to Moses, 'We promise that we'll do everything God wants us to do!' So Moses got busy. First, he wrote down all the laws God had given him. Then he built a stone altar in the shadow of Mount Sinai and he organised men to make special sacrifices and burnt offerings to God – they led all the best cows and sheep to the altar and slit their throats so that the blood gushed out like a bright red waterfall. Moses collected it up until he had rows and rows of bowls brimming with the animals' lifeblood.

Then Moses sealed the deal with God. He threw some of the blood at the altar until it was red and dripping. Then he read out the laws God had given him: these were the small print of God's treaty or covenant with his people. The people repeated their promise: 'We'll do everything God wants us to do!' Then – **SPLATTER SPLOOSH!** Moses threw all the rest of the blood over the people until they were sticky with gloopy gore. This bloodbath was a sign of the promise they'd made.

Finally Moses, his brother Aaron and a chosen few went right up to the top of the mountain. There was an awesome sight waiting for them: God himself was standing on a sapphire pavement and when they fell on their faces before him they could see right through the blue, crystal clear stone and down to the mountain below. It was as if they were standing on air! They could even see the Israelites far away like a crowd of tiny termites. Then God invited Moses, Aaron and the others to share a meal with him. Every mouthful of delicious food they shared at God's table reminded them of God's goodness and his awesome pact with them – he was their God and they were his special people.

After the meal, God said, 'Moses! Meet me on the mountain – I'll give you the commandments carved in stone, so that your people can keep them for ever.' So Moses sent Aaron and the chosen few to look after the Israelites while he went to meet God on the mountain.

WOOOOOMPF! A fierce wildfire appeared on top of Mount Sinai – it showed everyone that God's glory had arrived there once more. A thick cloud surrounded the fire, and the Israelites strained their eyes to see Moses, like a tiny black dot, disappearing into the cloud to meet God. That was the last they saw of him for a very long time.

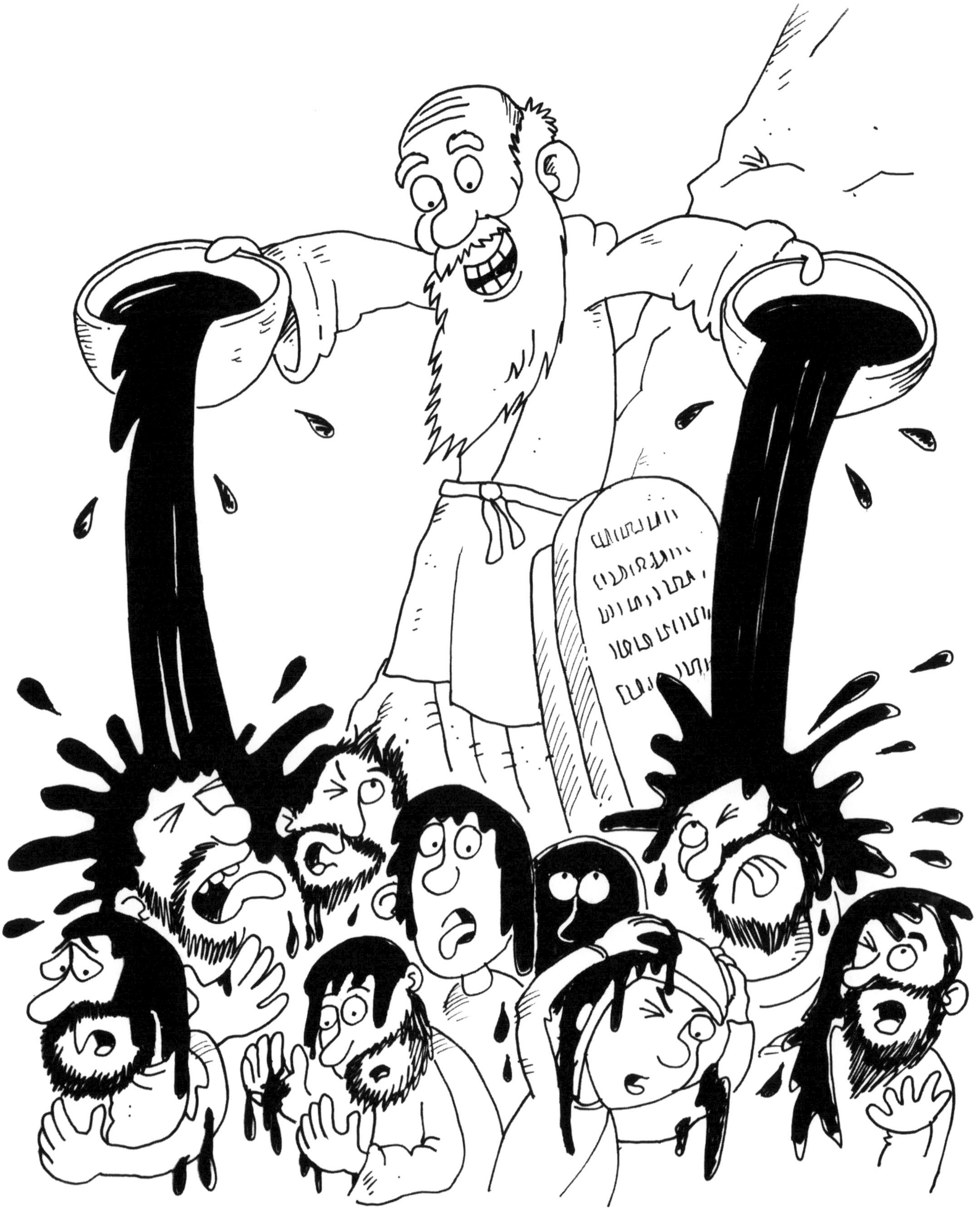

Bad behaviour and disgusting drinks

The people waited for Moses. As the hours stretched into days and the days became weeks, they said to each other, 'Is he ever coming back? Is he dead? What's he doing? Where's God?' They remembered the gods back in Egypt – those beautiful golden animal statues that the people worshipped – and they wished they had a god they could get close to, instead of hanging around a mountain for a holy man who might never come back. They went to Moses' brother, Aaron, and said, 'Make us a god we can worship!'

Can you remember what God's Rule number two was? That's right –

'Don't worship statues or idols or anything else that you've made yourselves.'

You remembered it, I'm sure, but – **OOPS** – Aaron and all the other leaders forgot it. In less time than it takes to recite the rest of the Ten Commandments, Aaron gathered up all the people's gold jewellery. Then he melted it down and shaped it into a statue of a calf. He showed it to the people and they said, 'The golden calf is god!' So Aaron built an altar for the calf and declared that the next day would be the calf's festival. **'HOORAY!'** shouted the Israelites, because everyone loves a festival.

The next day they made sacrifices to the calf and then got down to the serious business of eating, drinking and dancing. It was the biggest party they'd had since they left Egypt and it got wilder and wilder until God, high up on the mountain with Moses, heard the racket.

God roared at Moses, 'Just look what your people are doing! They've forgotten my laws already! Have you ever seen anyone so **STUBBORN?!** Now get out of my way so that I can blast them and burn them all up!'

Moses said, 'Please, Lord! Don't do it! Remember how you rescued your people from Egypt! Remember the promises you made to Abraham, Isaac and Jacob!* You said their families would grow and live for ever in the land you promised them!'

God listened to Moses and decided on a different plan. He said to Moses, 'It's time to go back to your people.' He gave Moses two stone tablets to carry, onto which God himself had carved his own laws.

So after 40 long, hot days and 40 long, cold nights on the mountain, Moses returned to the people he'd left behind. As he lugged the heavy stones down the mountain, he heard such a hullabaloo coming from the Israelite camp that he thought the people were getting ready for a battle. When he got closer, he couldn't believe his eyes or ears – wild dancing! Loud singing! Rude shouting! Food fights! And in the middle of it all there was a golden statue of a calf surrounded by sacrifices and grovelling people.

* You can read about these promises in *The human sacrifice* and *Tricky twins* in **Beastly Bible Stories 3**.

Moses was absolutely furious. He threw down God's stone tablets and they broke into pieces on the rocks of Mount Sinai. Then he shoved through the crowd and pushed over the golden calf statue – **CRASH!** In a rage he made some disgusting drinks: here's his recipe.

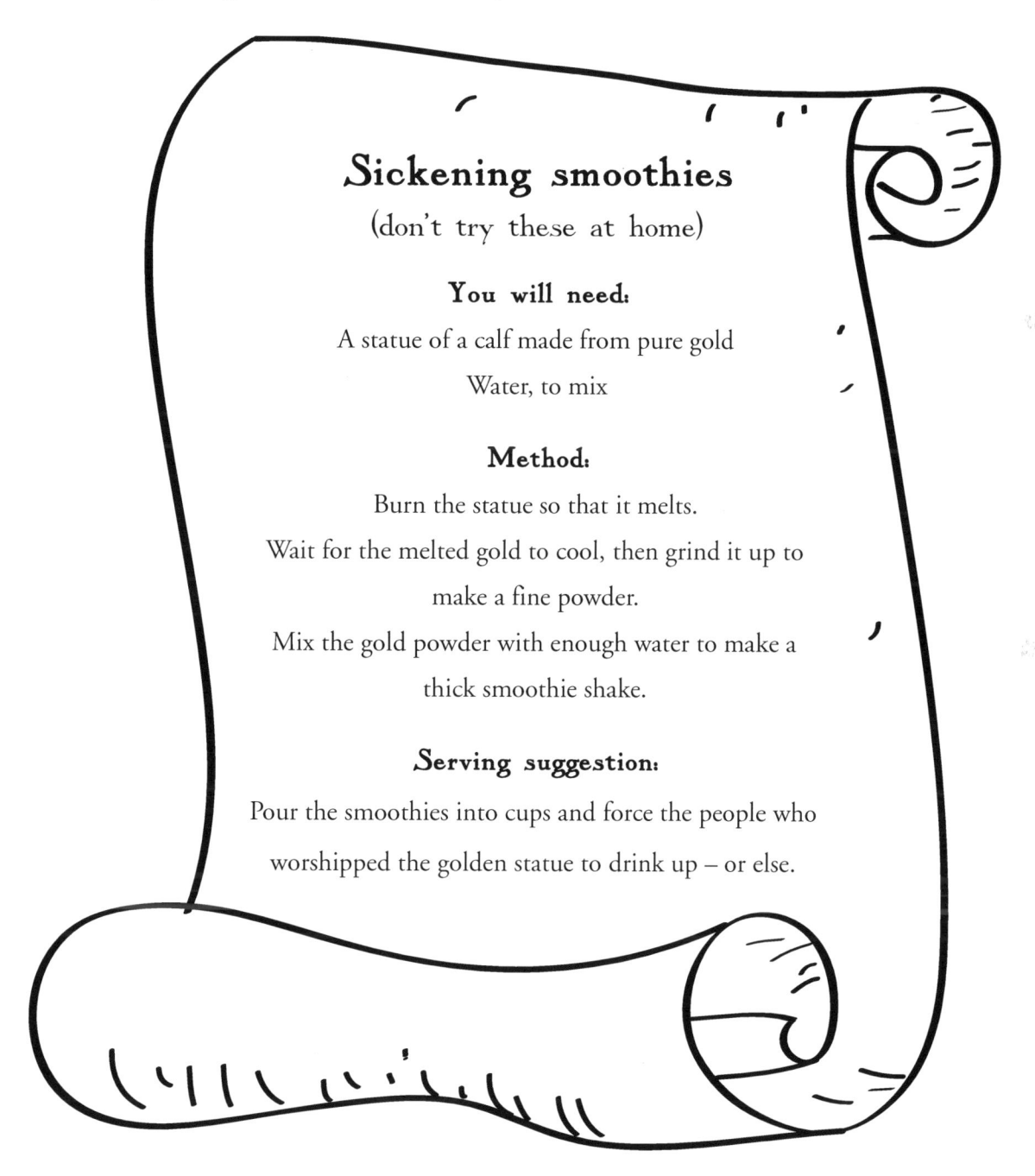

Sickening smoothies
(don't try these at home)

You will need:
A statue of a calf made from pure gold
Water, to mix

Method:
Burn the statue so that it melts.
Wait for the melted gold to cool, then grind it up to make a fine powder.
Mix the gold powder with enough water to make a thick smoothie shake.

Serving suggestion:
Pour the smoothies into cups and force the people who worshipped the golden statue to drink up – or else.

Aaron tried to explain to his brother what had happened, but Moses saw that the people were running wild and this was a time for action, not words. He stood up and shouted, 'Who's on God's side? Come here!' The members of his own tribe* recognised a battle cry when they heard it and they all rallied round. Moses gave them a terrifying order: 'Kill everyone who disobeyed God, even if you have to kill your friends and family!' They raced through the Israelite camp, swords slashing to left and right, and by the time the sun went down that night, 3000 Israelites lay dead in the desert.

Some people who had worshipped the golden calf breathed a sigh of relief that they had survived – **PHEW!** – but they didn't escape punishment. God sent a disgusting, deadly disease to finish them off.

The future looks bright

God told Moses to get his people ready for the rest of their journey through the desert. They were still his people, and he gave them an angel to lead them into battle against all their enemies, but he kept his distance. The Israelites were very sad – they felt as if God wasn't speaking to them any more. God only spoke to Moses, and eventually Moses said, 'We miss you, Lord. Everything is pointless unless you're with us.'

God listened to Moses and said, 'Very well. I will be with you and your people – my people.'

* Remember, there were 12 tribes of Israel.

Moses asked for one more thing: 'Lord, I want to see you face to face. Show me your glory.'

God said, 'If you see me face to face, you'll die. But come to the mountain tomorrow with two new stone tablets and I'll come as close as I can.'

The next morning, Moses did as he was told and climbed the mountain. God guided him to a man-sized crack in the rocks and said, 'I'm coming – look away now.' So God in all his glory came close to Moses, and Moses felt a gust of wind like a firm hand on his back push him into the crack in the rocks. When the wind dropped and Moses could move again, he peeped over his shoulder and saw the edge of God's glory, like the fiery brightness on the horizon just after the sun has gone down. Then a soft cloud wrapped itself around Moses and the mountain top, and God came to him in the cloud. God said, '**I AM THE LORD**! I am loving and forgiving and fair. These are my commandments.'

God reminded Moses of the Ten Commandments and carved his words into the new stone tablets. Then he said to Moses, 'This is my promise. Your people are my special people and I will do **AWESOME** things for you!'

So the covenant was mended and Moses stayed on the mountain with God for another 40 days and 40 nights without food or drink, and the Israelites waited for him. No one suggested a golden statue or planned a wild party this time. At last Moses came down from Mount Sinai carrying the Ten Commandments which were carved on two shiny, new, stone tablets. They weren't the only shiny thing – Moses' face was gleaming so brightly that it hurt the Israelites' eyes when they looked at him. It was as if he'd been close to God for so long that some of God's glory had rubbed off on him like glitter. In the end, because no one had yet invented sunglasses, Moses wore a veil to protect the Israelites' eyes from the glorious glare.

The Ten Commandments are the basis of Jewish religious law. God gave them to his people so that they would know how to behave properly and live well together. The first four commandments are about loving God and the rest are about loving each other. Jesus told his followers to keep the commandments, so they are important for Christians, too.

You can read the story of the Ten Commandments in Exodus chapters 19, 20, 24, 32–34.

CLEAN AND UNCLEAN
Rules for eating

On the menu

'Mum, I'm hungry – what can I have to eat?' whined the little boy. He was hot, thirsty and tired of walking on stony sand. He wasn't the only one. All God's special people, the Israelites, were travelling together through the desert* and they kept thinking about food, as you do on long journeys. God was looking after his people like a dad caring for his kids and – as parents do – he decided what they were allowed to eat. Now your parents might have rules about eating up all your greens and not scoffing too many sweets; God had rules for his children, too. When they were in the desert, he gave them a detailed set of rules that told them exactly what they were allowed to eat, which foods were forbidden and how food had to be prepared. Lots of different foods were OK with God: Jews today call these *kosher*. Here's what was on the menu for the Israelites (and for many traditional Jewish families today).

---

* You can find out why the Israelites were in the desert in the first place by reading *Blood, bugs and boils*, *Blood on the door* and *Walking under the waves* in **Beastly Bible Stories 4**.

Menu

Beef or lamb
(or any other animals that eat grass and have divided hooves)

Fish
(with fins and scales)

Chicken

Locusts
(or crickets or grasshoppers)

Served with any of the following*:

Eggs

Grain

Nuts**

Vegetables

Fruit

Dairy products (milk, cheese, etc.)
will be served a few hours after the meat course.

*Suitable for vegetarians

**Warning – may contain nuts

Hands off!

Lots of things were off the menu. The Israelites weren't allowed to eat anything with paws. They couldn't nibble anything creepy or crawly, such as insects, snakes or lizards. Pigs were a forbidden food, so that ruled out roast pork, ham, gammon, bacon, sausages and pork scratchings. Lots of less tasty things were also banned, such as birds of prey: no hawk pies for the Israelites.

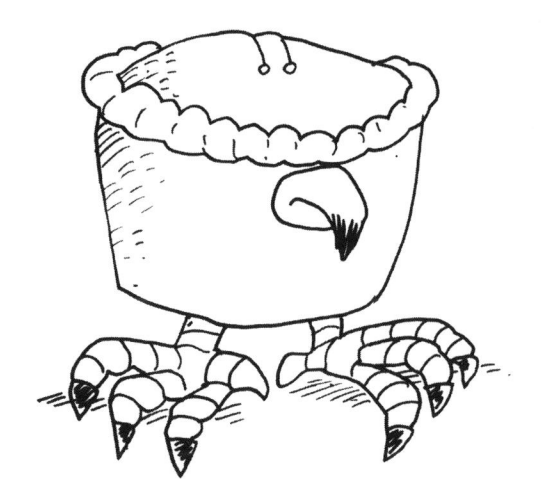

Camel casserole was not kosher because camels had the wrong kind of hooves.

Jellyfish jelly was not allowed because jellyfish don't have fins or scales.

Blood was definitely banned because blood keeps all creatures alive – it's their lifeblood.* So bat burgers with blood ketchup were out of the question.

* Meat isn't kosher unless a clean animal is killed in a special way so that the blood drains out of the body before it is chopped up into steaks and joints.

Keeping clean

God's food rules were more than dos and don'ts. The rules said that the good foods were **CLEAN** and the forbidden foods were **UNCLEAN** – the Bible uses the word 'detestable', which told the Jews to *hate* these unclean foods. God wanted his people to keep their hands off certain foods and he wanted them to be clean, but why?

Well, you know how parents nag kids to wash their hands before they tuck into their dinner? That's because they don't want anyone getting an upset tummy. God looked after the Israelites like a parent and he gave them rules about cleanness partly to keep them healthy, because he wanted his special people to survive. Pork is a dodgy meat to keep in the desert because it quickly turns magotty, so the Israelites were definitely better off without it. Mixing meat and milk isn't a good idea in hot weather, because the milk goes manky and the meat goes mouldy, so God told his people to keep these things apart.*

Here's another example of the Bible's food rules: if a dead mouse dropped on your wooden chopping board, you had to wash the chopping board and leave it to dry in the sun until bedtime (sensible, really). If you found a dead lizard in your pot of flour or your water jug, you had to chuck out the flour or the water and the jug as well (just to be on the safe side). These laws were a bit like modern hygiene rules for keeping food fresh and kitchens clean.

---

* Today, traditional Jewish kitchens still have separate areas for meat and dairy products, each with their own pots and pans. Meaty and milky foods are never served together – if you'd eaten roast beef for dinner, you wouldn't be allowed ice cream for pudding until several hours afterwards.

God had another reason for wanting his people to be clean: they were his special people and he told them, 'I am your God. I'm holy, so you must be holy.' For his people, being holy meant being good on the inside and clean on the outside. It was a bit like having to wash behind your ears, put on your smartest clothes and be on your best behaviour for a special family occasion. When the Israelites followed the rules about clean and unclean food, it was their way of showing that they were good, holy and special to God.

In Moses' time, when the Israelites were surrounded by all sorts of tribes and nations, the food rules made them different from other people. Throughout the history of the Jewish people, sticking to the food rules – keeping kosher – has been a sign of Jewish belonging. Today the food rules are still followed by traditional Jewish families across the world.

You can read about the food rules in Leviticus chapter 11.

BLOOD AND GUTS
Rules for sacrificing animals

God goes camping

'WOOOAAHH! Look at **THAT**!' The boys were wide awake although it was long past their bedtime. They peered out of their family's tent and gawped at the towering column of fire that ripped apart the night sky like a giant lightsaber. In its glow they could see the tents of their refugee camp stretching in every direction, and faces appearing round every tent flap to look at this new wonder. All day there had been a strange, swirling pillar of cloud hovering above their campsite. Now that it was dark – and in the desert, the nights are very dark – the cloudy pillar had suddenly burst into flame.

'**GOD'S TENT IS ON FIRE!**' shouted the boys' big sister when she saw what was going on. She pointed at the special tent that God's people had finished building that very day. It was lit up by the fire but – miraculously – it wasn't burning. The tent was quite a sight: it had carved wooden pillars and was draped with gorgeously coloured curtains; everything inside it glowed with gold and shone with jewels. Behind the finest curtain of all stood the precious Ark of the Covenant – the box that contained the stone tablets of the Ten Commandments. The tent was called the *tent of meeting* or *the tabernacle* and it was God's special place. After everything that he and his people had been through together,* he had decided to come and live with them in their desert campsite in his own special tent. The strange cloud and the weird fire above the tent showed the people that God in all his glory was at home.

Bloodbath

How would *you* get ready to meet God in his special tent? Perhaps you'd have a good wash and put on your best clothes as you would for a special guest. You might want to give him the best present you could afford, just like you'd give your mum or dad a special birthday present. You might be on your best behaviour, as if your head teacher were coming to tea (Imagine!). You might even want to make up for any bad behaviour that you felt sad or worried about. Meeting God in his special tent must have been like all these things rolled into one, and then some. It was a big deal. So God gave his people some rules about what they had to do when they came to his tent.

---

* They had been through quite a lot, as you'll discover if you read *Blood, bugs and boils*, *Blood on the door* and *Walking under the waves* in **Beastly Bible Stories 4**. These stories explain why God's people became refugees and desert campers in the first place.

ANIMAL SACRIFICE – there's no nice way of putting it. Blood, guts and gore were the most important part of worshipping God when his people were in the desert, and for many years afterwards. Animals were sacrificed for lots of different reasons.

WARNING

CONTAINS VIOLENCE
ANIMALS WERE HARMED IN THE MAKING OF THIS STORY

- ☑ Dedicated to God?
- ☑ Making peace with God, your family or your community?
- ☑ Thanking God?
- ☑ Saying sorry to God?
- ☑ Saying sorry to other people?

YOU NEED

ANIMAL SACRIFICE

* Terms and conditions apply (see below). Offer valid until 70 AD.

God gave detailed rules for sacrificing animals and they varied depending on the reason for the sacrifice. For example, here's what you would have to do if you'd been bad and you wanted God to forgive your sins:

1. Find a perfect animal – a bull if you're very rich, a sheep if you're not quite so well off or a dove if you're broke. (Only the best will do – don't fob God off with a three-legged sheep.)
2. Go to the entrance of the courtyard that surrounds God's tent. Right in front of you there will be a big shiny altar with a fire burning on it – this is the altar of burnt offering. Put your hand on your animal's head. (This shows that the animal is your stand-in for the sacrifice – it'll die for your sins instead of you. Phew.)
3. Kill it (cut its throat if it's an animal or wring its neck if it's a bird).
4. The priest must collect the blood and dip his finger in it, then sprinkle blood seven times in front of the curtains surrounding God's tent.
5. The priest must take some of the blood into the tent, where there is a second altar for burning incense* – it has pointy corners like horns. The priest must smear some of the blood on the horns of this altar (to make it pure and holy).
6. The priest must pour the rest of the blood around the altar of burnt offering.

* Incense looks a bit like grit or gravel but when it burns it makes white, sweet-smelling smoke which reminds people of holiness.

7. The priest must fish around in the dead animal's guts and pull out all the fat, including the liver and the kidneys and their floppy, fatty coverings. If it's a sheep, he must cut off its fatty tail and bottom. These are the best bits, so he must sacrifice them to God.

8. Burn all the fatty bits on the altar. (God likes the smell of roasting meat.)

9. The rest of the meat may be eaten by the priests, but no one is allowed to eat any fat or any blood.

10. All the leftovers get dumped on a bonfire outside the camp and burned (including the head, skin, flesh, legs, guts and dung).

Getting right with God

The Bible is soaked with animal blood from the very beginning – Adam and Eve's children fell out over a sacrifice,* and you'll remember that the first thing Noah did after the flood was to thank God by killing a crowd of the animals he'd rescued.* So what's it all about?

Sacrifice is about dealing with what the Bible calls sin. People are always messing up, getting things wrong and being bad – we're only human. But God wants us to be good: he said to his people in the desert, 'I am your God. I'm holy,

---

* You can read their story in *Killer Cain* in **Beastly Bible Stories 3**.
** Read *The fatal flood* earlier in this book.

BEFORE	AFTER

so you must be holy.' Sacrifice was a way of getting rid of sin and getting right with God. It worked like this:

- **Only the best will do.** Sacrifice meant giving the best to God. Animals were precious possessions in those days and people only killed them on very special occasions, such as a wedding or a festival. Killing an animal for God was like giving him a really special present, and killing the most perfect animal was the best present you could afford.
- **Paying the price.** The sacrificed animal was a stand-in for the sinner. If you'd been so bad that you deserved to die, the animal you offered would die in your place.
- **A bloodbath.** In the Bible, the blood of all creatures is special. It is described as the source of life, the lifeblood. The blood of a sacrificed animal is sometimes seen as an offering which will unite people with God. It's also a kind of holy cleanser which makes God's people, tent and altars pure and holy.

The Jews continued to make animal sacrifices for more than 1300 years until the Romans destroyed the Temple in Jerusalem in 70 AD. However, the Jews who followed Jesus stopped sacrificing after he died on the cross, because they saw Jesus himself as the final blood sacrifice. These first Christians understood his gory death in the same way as they understood the sacrifices that had been part of their worship for centuries – like this:

- ***Only the best will do.** Jesus was perfect, like the best sheep in the flock that was chosen for sacrifice.*
- ***Paying the price.** Jesus was a stand-in for sinners – he paid the price for everyone's badness by dying.*
- ***A bloodbath.** It sounds gruesome to us, but to the first Christians Jesus' blood was like the animals' blood that poured down the altars in the desert – it washed away sins and brought people close to God by making them pure and holy. Jesus was like the sacrificed animal, and also like the priest who made the sacrifice for the people's sake.*

Christians today still understand Jesus' death as a sacrifice – that's why Jesus is sometimes called 'the lamb of God'.

You can read the rules for sacrificing animals in Leviticus chapters 1-7.

HAIR-RAISING HORROR

THE HORRIBLE HAIRCUT
Samson loses his strength

Hide and seek

Do you remember Samson? Of course you do – he was the big Israelite bloke who was born to beat his people's enemies, the Philistines. When God's Spirit gave Samson super strength, he was stronger than the Incredible Hulk. He had legs like tree trunks, a six-pack like armour, and pigtails. That's right – Strongman Samson had long, frizzy hair which he wore in plaits, because an angel had told his mum that he must never, ever have a haircut.

In the first half of Samson's story,* he wrestled with a lion, set fire to foxes and finished off Philistines by the dozen. After attacks and counter-attacks, Samson was in the lead at half time, but the battle wasn't over yet.

Out in the desert, Samson crunched across the Philistine bones that were left over from their last fight and headed for a hiding place in the hills. He tucked himself away in a cave and spent the rest of the afternoon picking his enemies'

---

* You can read the first half of Samson's story in *Wrestling with lions and setting fire to foxes* in **Beastly Bible Stories 1**.

blood from between his fingers and toes, then he settled down for a doze. Being his people's champion was hard work.

Meanwhile, the surviving Philistines were on the warpath. They wanted revenge. They attacked a local tribe and tore their camp apart looking for Samson until there were tattered tents, dead donkeys and crying kids everywhere – but no Samson. The tribesmen knew where he was hiding, so 3000 of them set off straight away to have a word with him.

'WHAT HAVE YOU DONE TO ANNOY THE PHILISTINES?!' they yelled.

Samson shrugged. 'They started it.'

'We don't want any trouble here!' the men replied. 'We're handing you over to the Philistines!'

They agreed not to hurt Samson, so he let them tie him up. They bound his hands and arms with brand new ropes that looked strong enough to hold an elephant, then they dragged him back to the Philistines who were still rampaging through their camp.

Lethal weapon

'**YEEEAAAAAAAHHHHH!**' The Philistines let out a great triumphant yell when they saw Samson tied up with ropes like a gift-wrapped gorilla. They surged towards him but at that very moment, God sent his Spirit's super strength to Samson and – **WOOOOMPF!** – the ropes around him melted like a cheestrings on a barbecue. Samson grabbed the nearest weapon that came to hand – a jawbone from a dead donkey (freshly killed by the Philistines) with teeth and gums still attached.

'**ATTAAAAAAAAACK!**' roared Samson and, armed with the jawbone, he charged at the Philistines. **SLASH! CRUNCH! SMASH! BAM!** Samson murdered men to his left and right. He killed the ones who came at him from the front and slaughtered the ones who tried to sneak up from behind.

When Samson had finished, 1000 Philistines lay dead. Samson chucked the jawbone over his shoulder and looked at the bodies in front of him. Then he realised something: all this fighting in the desert had made him desperate for a drink. He prayed to God, 'Lord, you gave me this victory! Now please don't let me die of thirst!'

God heard Samson and – **BAM!** – he split open a hollow in the ground and fresh water sprang from it. '**GLUG-GLUG-GLUG-GLUG!**' Samson drank and drank until he felt like himself again. On that day he became his people's leader – or judge – and he stayed in charge of the Israelites for 20 years.

The horrible haircut

Samson was always on the lookout for love. He had tried to get married once, but it hadn't worked out. His wife-to-be and her dad were burned alive by the Philistines, so Samson was still single.

GreatDate.com

Tall, dark, handsome hero with super strength WLTM gorgeous girl for romance and possible marriage. Could you love a man with muscles and plaits? Contact Samson the Israelite.

One woman who caught Samson's eye was Delilah. She was a Philistine but she was also a dark-haired beauty and he fell head over heels in love with her. When the Philistines saw Samson hanging about Delilah's tent with a lovesick look on his face, they came up with a plan to defeat their enemy for good. The Philistine lords paid Delilah a visit and made her an offer she couldn't refuse: 'Find out his secret! Trick him into telling you where he gets his super strength from, so that we can beat him. Then each of us will give you more than 1000 silver coins.'

That was a big bribe, but Delilah wasn't fooled. She remembered the last woman the lords had visited with an offer she couldn't refuse: they had told his first wife-to-be to trick Samson, too, or else they'd burn her and her dad alive – and that's exactly what they'd done in the end. Delilah was very frightened. On one side she faced the rich lords who had the power to get rid of anyone – and on the other side she faced Samson the strongman, who at the moment was following her around like a faithful puppy. She decided that Samson would be easier to deal with.

'Oooh, Samson,' she cooed, stroking his muscly arms. 'You're so big and strong! I wish you'd tell me the secret of your strength.'

Samson just smiled.

'Let's play a game,' Delilah purred. 'Tell me how to tie you up so you can't escape, and I'll pretend I'm an army coming to attack you!' Delilah playfully put on a feather-topped Philistine helmet. (It rather suited her.)

Samson liked the idea of Delilah dressing up and playing soldiers with him, so he played along. 'There's only one way to tie me up so that I can't escape: you need to use seven fresh bowstrings.'

Delilah popped into the room next door, where a gang of heavily armed Philistine soldiers were lying in wait. They gave her seven fresh bowstrings and she put her finger to her lips: 'Sshh!' Then she tiptoed back to Samson and tied him up with the bowstrings.

Delilah put on her helmet and shouted, 'The Philistines are coming!' Samson simply flexed his muscles and snapped the bowstrings like spider's thread. He roared with laughter and Delilah pretended to laugh too, but her heart sank because she hadn't found out the secret of his strength.

So Delilah tried again. 'Oooh, you big fibber! Please tell me how to tie you up so you can't escape!'

Samson liked this game. 'There's only one way to tie me up so that I can't escape: you need to use brand-new ropes.'

Delilah popped into the room next door again and the gang of soldiers gave her several coils of new rope. She crossed her fingers for luck then she tiptoed back to Samson and tied him up with the ropes.

Delilah put on her helmet again and shouted, 'The Philistines are coming!' Samson simply flexed his muscles and snapped the ropes like spaghetti. He roared with laughter and Delilah pretended to laugh too, but her tummy began to tie itself in knots because she still hadn't found out the secret of his strength.

'Stop teasing me!' pouted Delilah. 'Please tell me how to tie you up so you can't escape!'

Samson was enjoying all this attention. 'There's only one way to tie me up so that I can't escape: you need to weave my plaits into your loom.'

While the soldiers waited impatiently in the room next door, Delilah made Samson a bed of cushions next to her loom, on which she was weaving some brightly coloured cloth. Samson sighed happily and dozed on the cushions as Delilah gently wove back and forth, back and forth, until Samson's plaits were part of the pattern of her cloth and he was stuck fast.

Then Delilah put on her helmet once more and shouted, 'The Philistines are coming!' Samson woke up, shook his head and broke the loom into bits. His plaits sprang free like escaping snakes and he laughed even harder. Delilah felt sick because she still hadn't found out the secret of his strength and the soldiers next door were getting restless.

So Delilah got cross with Samson: 'How can you say "I love you"? I don't think you love me at all, because you've lied to me three times now and you still won't trust me with the secret of your strength. Please, please tell me!'

'No,' replied Samson.

'If you really loved me, you'd tell me.'

'No way.'

'Oh go on – you can trust little me.'

'It's a secret.'

'Please!'

'No way!' – and so on, for days and days, until finally:

'Please, please, please, please, **PLEASE** tell me your secret!'

'OH ALL RIGHT! JUST STOP NAGGING ME!' Delilah's pester power had triumphed.

'Here's my secret,' sighed Samson. 'I must never shave my hair off – God sent an angel to tell my mum that when she was expecting me. If I shave my head, I'll lose all my strength.'

'PHEW!' Delilah and Samson each let out a huge sigh of relief – she'd finally got what she wanted and he could have some peace and quiet at last. He rested his head in her lap and dropped off to sleep.

Then things happened fast. Delilah called a servant to shave off all Samson's hair while he slept. When his head was bald and bristly she shouted, 'The Philistines are coming!' Samson woke up, thinking she was playing their game again, but strong hands suddenly grabbed his arms and legs and thick ropes secured his hands. He didn't panic – he simply flexed his muscles. **NOTHING**

HAPPENED. He was as weak as a weedy wimp. The soldiers bundled him out of the room and he felt the breeze on his bare head. *Then* he panicked – he realised that Delilah had betrayed him and God's super strength had left him.

The Philistine lords paid Delilah the thousands of silver coins they had promised her, but no amount of money could stop her feeling sorry for what she'd done to Samson. Meanwhile, the Philistines made the most of having Samson in their power: first they poked out his eyes – **SQUISH, SQUELCH**. Then they put him in prison and chained him up with bronze shackles. As a final insult, they gave him a donkey's job – they made him turn the prison's mill to grind their flour. Day after day, Samson trudged round in a circle wearing a heavy harness. But – millimetre by millimetre – his shaved hair began to grow back . . .

Samson's revenge

The Philistines held a big party in their great hall. They began with a sacrifice to their god to say thank you for Samson's capture, then they had a massive feast and a wild celebration. 'Hooray!' they shouted. 'He murdered our men and now he's milling our flour!' When the party was in full swing, the Philistine lords decided it would be a good joke to bring Samson up to the party in his chains so that they could all laugh at him. 'Down with Samson the weakling! Down with blind, baldie Samson!' the people jeered as guards were sent to fetch the prize prisoner.

Samson stumbled in, led by his guards, with two empty holes where his eyes used to be. They stood him between the two central pillars that held up the hall's roof, where everyone could see him. Samson asked them to let him touch the pillars so he could lean on them if he felt tired. Everyone cheered when they saw how feeble he looked, and some people threw rotten fruit and bread rolls at him. In fact, they were so busy jeering and laughing at him that no one noticed that there was something different about Samson: his head wasn't bald any more. During the months he had been in prison, his hair had grown back. It wasn't neatly plaited, of course – it had grown into a wild, frizzy bush – but it was definitely long.

Samson listened to the cheering of the Philistine men and women and the boasting of the Philistine lords. There were thousands of party guests inside the great hall, and another 3000 on the roof that was held up by the great pillars. Samson leaned against the pillars and prayed, 'God, please give me super strength this one last time. I want to pay these people back for taking my eyes.' Then Samson flexed his muscles and leaned his full weight on the two pillars and – miraculously – God sent his Spirit's super strength. **'LET ME DIE WITH THIS LOT!'** yelled Samson, and pushed **HARD.**

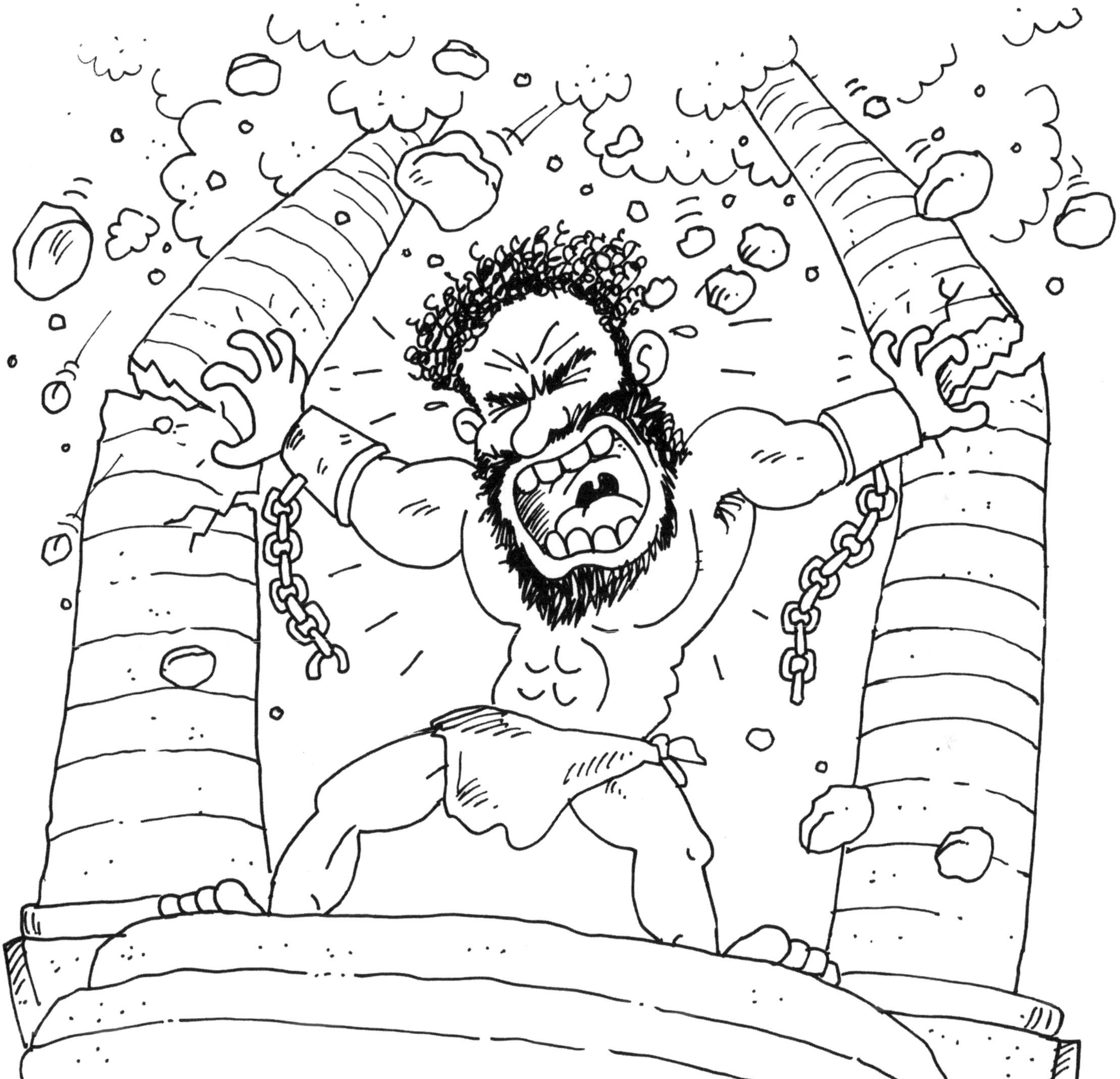

CRAAAAAAACK – CRAAAASSSSHHHHHHH – THUUUUDDDD! The pillars cracked and toppled over, then the roof, weighed down by 3000 people, collapsed into the hall.

'**AAAAIIIIEEEEEEEE!**' screamed the party guests inside and the party guests on the roof as the building crashed down around them. Stones fell on people and people fell on stones until every single person was killed: all the Philistine lords, all their party guests and – of course – Samson himself. In his final act, he finished off more Philistines than he had killed in his whole life.

When Samson was buried, Israel mourned the man who been their judge for 20 years and the hero who had fought back against the Philistines, as the angel had promised his mum he would.

Samson is a big Bible hero, but you have to admit that he didn't always behave well. His battles were very bloodthirsty and he was obsessed with getting his own back, yet God still chose him to be his people's champion against the Philistines, and God gave him super strength when he needed it. In Samson's stories, God is clearly the big boss who is completely in charge and is always working for his people's good. Later, when God promised his people a Saviour, many of them must have hoped for a hero like Samson the strongman – but God sent Jesus instead, who was very different, as you'll find out in **Beastly Bible Stories – The Terrific New Testament.**

You can read about Samson's horrible haircut in Judges chapters 15 and 16.

A TERRIBLE TANGLE
The death of Absalom

Drop-dead gorgeous

You know how some people are ridiculously good-looking? Absalom, the son of King David,* was like that: tall, dark-eyed and impossibly, eye-wateringly handsome. He was perfect from the top of his square-jawed head to the soles of his suntanned feet. If there had been a prize in those days for Israel's Next Top Model, Absalom would have won it with every vote. His crowning glory was his hair, which he wore very long and beautifully curled in the latest fashion. He only cut it once a year, when it was too hot and heavy for his head, and he was so proud of his lovely locks that he liked to weigh them. The last lot weighed more than 2kg!

However, Absalom wasn't happy. In fact, he was furious. First he'd killed his horrible half-brother in revenge for an awful attack on his sister, and then he'd been banned from Jerusalem for three years. When he finally wangled his way

---

* You can read about David's adventures before he became king in *The giant killer* in **Beastly Bible Stories 1**.

back into the city, his father, King David, refused to see him. They didn't speak for two more years. Absalom's blood boiled: this was no way to treat a royal prince who had every right to become king! So he gave an order to his servants: 'Bring me Joab, the commander of my father's army! He must make my father see me.' The message was sent, but Joab refused to come. So Absalom gave another order: 'Burn down Joab's field of barley! That'll teach him to ignore me!'

WOOOOMPF-CRACKLE-CRACKLE! Joab's field of barley – all his family's food for the winter – went up in smoke.

'WHY HAVE YOUR SERVANTS BURNED DOWN MY BARLEY?' demanded Joab, who had leapt out of bed and dashed straight to Absalom's house when he heard the bad news.

'I thought that would get your attention,' sneered Absalom. 'Now get me in to see the king!'

So Joab spoke to King David and the king sent for Absalom. There were tears and apologies and finally a reunion between father and son – hugs and kisses all round. At last Absalom was back where he felt he belonged – in his father's good books, in the royal palace and in line for the throne.

Everyone's favourite

Absalom had a plan: he wanted to be king instead of his dad, without waiting for David to die of old age. Absalom felt he had waited long enough, so he started to behave like a Very Important Person. He got himself a chariot (very shiny, the latest model) and he got himself an entourage (a big gang of bodyguards and assistants, just like modern celebrities have). Absalom never went anywhere without his flashy chariot pulled by fine horses and surrounded by 50 men. He wore his finest clothes and made sure his hair looked particularly handsome. Men envied him and women gasped, 'Oh, isn't he gorgeous! Just look at his lovely long hair!'

For the next stage of his plan, Absalom relied on his good looks, charm and ruthless cunning. Every day he got up early and stood beside the main road into Jerusalem. As people arrived at the city with questions for the king and problems for him to solve, Absalom got to them first with a handsome grin and a cheery handshake, as if meeting them had made his day. 'What's your name?' he'd ask them. 'Where are you from?' Wherever they came from and whichever Israelite tribe they belonged to, Absalom always had a story to tell and a memory to share. 'You're from Geshur!' he'd say. 'That's where my mum's family comes from! Ah, I've spent some happy times there – I remember those hills. On a clear day you can see forever! Mind you, I remember the time I lost my neighbour's donkey up there . . .'

Absalom made people smile, laugh and chat – in other words, he charmed the pants off them. When they felt like old friends, he'd ask them about the problem they had brought for the king to solve. He'd listen carefully and then shake his head. 'Ah, what a shame! It could all be so easily sorted out, but the king is too busy to listen to you! Now, if I were in charge here, I'd make time for everyone to come and see me, and I'd sort out problems like yours straight away. Still, David is the king – what can I do?' And he'd leave his new fan to think about that question as he went to shake the next person's hand.

Father vs son

After four years of being chatty, charming and cunning, Absalom had won over so many people that he was Israel's favourite. Everyone loved him more than they loved King David, and he knew that the time had come for him to take his dad's throne.

Absalom announced to the king, 'I'm going to worship God in Hebron!' (Hebron was David's second-best capital city.)

'Good boy,' said King David.

However, Absalom secretly sent messages to all his supporters in Israel: 'When you hear the trumpets, tell everyone: "Long live Absalom, king of Hebron!"'

When he reached Hebron and his army blew their trumpets, Absalom's fans from all over the country rushed to support him, hoping he'd soon be the handsome new king of Israel.

'Run away!' shouted King David to his court when he heard the news. 'Absalom will kill us all and flatten Jerusalem! **GET OUT NOW!**'

So while Absalom and his ever-growing army marched towards Jerusalem, David and his faithful supporters left the city and headed for the desert, crying as they went. As Absalom passed cheering crowds on his way into Jerusalem, an old man chucked stones at David and cursed him: 'This is all your fault!'

Absalom settled down to a victory feast in Jerusalem while his dad camped by the river Jordan and went to sleep feeling very sad, because he knew that the old man had a point* and that whatever happened now, it was up to God.

Meanwhile, God had a plan to deal with Absalom . . .

A terrible tangle

The next day, King David got ready for war. He organised his thousands of soldiers, appointed his commanders and armed them all for a fierce fight. 'I'll lead you into battle myself – I'll be in the front line!' he said.

---

* Find out what David had done wrong in *Killer king* in **Beastly Bible Stories 3**.

David's faithful captain, Joab, said, 'Your majesty, that would be unwise. They'd rather kill you than thousands of us! Please stay behind and send us reinforcements if we need them.'

'Very well,' said David.

Meanwhile, Absalom got his troops ready for war and said, 'Why don't we sneak up on my dad tonight with 12,000 men?'

Absalom's adviser was an undercover spy for King David. He said, 'Your majesty, that would be unwise. They might kill thousands of us! Please send for reinforcements and lead us into battle yourself – be in the front line!'

'Very well,' said Absalom. God's plan was working.

TRAMP TRAMP TRAMP TRAMP TRAMP TRAMP! Absalom led his thousands of marching men out to war against King David.

TRAMP TRAMP TRAMP TRAMP TRAMP TRAMP! King David's captains led thousands more men to meet them. David gave them one last order: 'Go easy on my son, Absalom. Be gentle with him.'

'CHAAAAAAAAAAAARGE!' Commanders on both sides gave the order and the two armies raced towards each other over rocks and through streams and across fields until they clashed in a forest where trees stood like lines of soldiers. The battle became a bloodthirsty game of hide and seek as soldiers dodged each other in and out of the shadows. Spears shot through the leafy branches, horses fell against tree trunks and archers climbed up high to get a better shot. David's army were winning as they left 20,000 dead men behind them in the forest and headed out into open country, still fighting.

Absalom had lost all his best men. He jumped on a mule which had been carrying provisions and kicked it hard, then headed back towards the forest to find a hiding place. He'd lost his sword and his helmet had fallen off in the fight, so his beautiful hair was flying wildly behind him as he raced away from David's army.

'THERE HE IS!' yelled one of David's soldiers. He chased after Absalom and was just in time to see what happened next. Absalom reached the edge of the forest and his mule galloped towards the thick, twisting branches of an ancient oak tree. The branches were low and the tangled twigs reached down like grasping fingers.

'NEARLY THERE!' shouted Absalom to his mule. **'KEEP CLEAR OF THE – WHUUUURP!'** As he rode under the lowest branches, the twigs twisted into Absalom's long hair and tangled it tightly. He was yanked straight off the mule, which galloped on without him. Absalom dangled from his hair and twisted furiously like a fly caught in a spider's web.

The soldier who saw all this remembered that King David had said, 'Go easy on my son, Absalom. Be gentle with him.' He ran back to his commander, Joab, and told him what he'd seen. Joab hadn't forgotten David's order, but he knew that there would never be any peace while Absalom lived. He also remembered his burned field of barley and his hungry children.

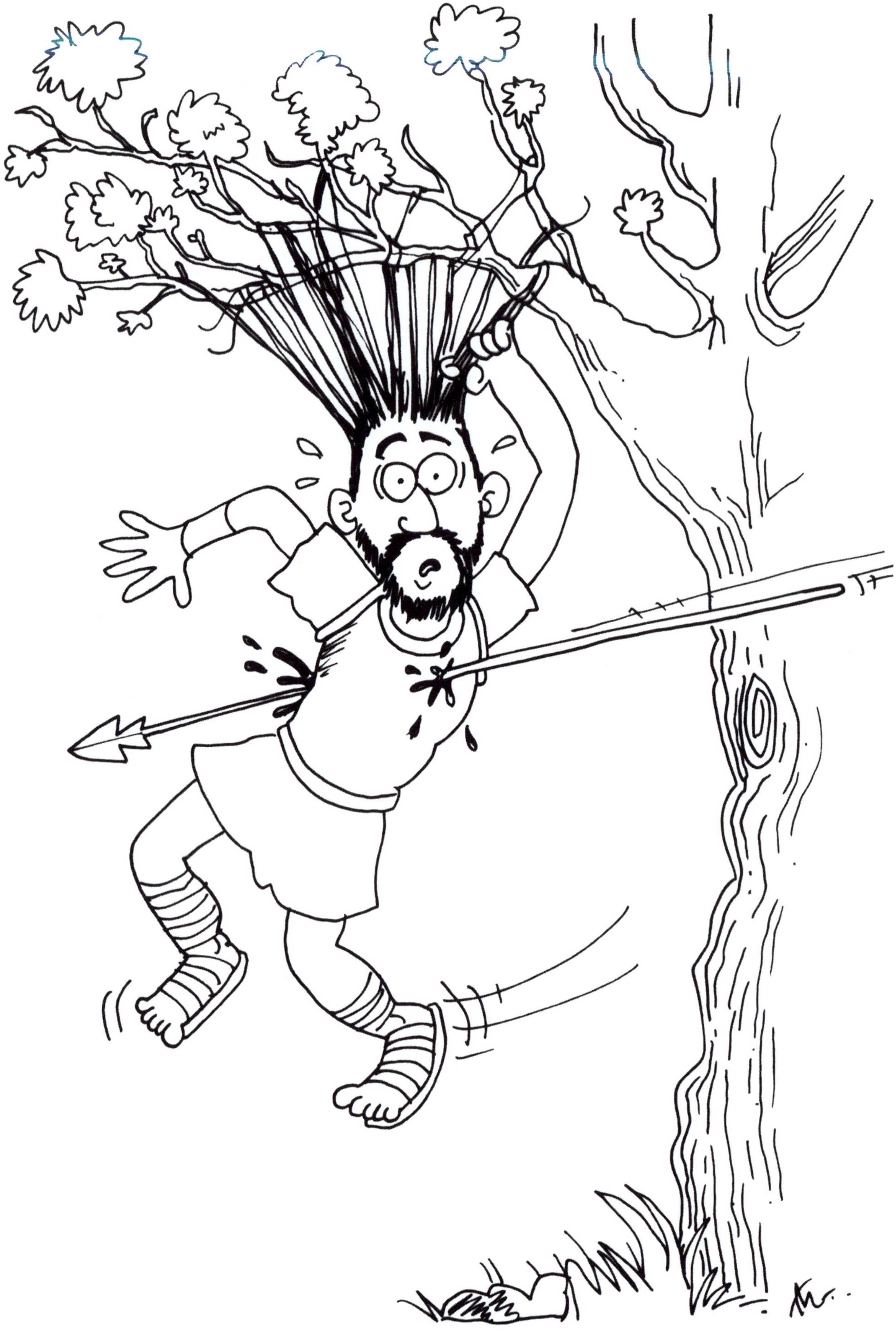

'Get out of my way!' shouted Joab to the soldier. 'It's time we finished this!'

Joab turned his horse towards the forest and galloped off, armed with three spears. He saw Absalom dangling from his tangled hair and took aim: **THUNK THUNK THUNK!** Three spears hit Absalom in the heart, then Joab sent ten of his men to finish him off. Finally they cut down his body, buried him in a big pit in the forest and laid a heap of stones over him, as if they were burying a common criminal and not a king's son.

When messengers arrived breathlessly in front of King David, they brought him good news and bad news. First the good news: 'Your majesty, your army has won!' Then the bad news: 'Your majesty, your son is dead!'

David wailed, 'Oh Absalom, my son! I wish I'd died instead of you!'

As you can imagine, this didn't go down very well with the soldiers who had fought hard, risked death and won the battle to save King David's life. 'There's no pleasing some people,' they grumbled.

David remained king but his reign was never easy. There was fighting between the tribes and Absalom wasn't the last of the king's sons to try and take the throne. Israel needed a great king to bring the tribes together and rule in peace – but everyone had to wait until David's son Solomon took the job.*

You can read about Absalom in 2 Samuel chapters 14–18.

---

* You can read about wise King Solomon in *Half a baby* in **Beastly Bible Stories 3**.